INSIDER'S VIEW:

DIALOGUES

ON

INTELLECTUAL
PROPERTY

IN CHINA

Editorial Board

Catherine Sun

Victor Xue

Consulting Editor

Dmitri Hubbard

Publisher

Abelle Yip

BBA

D1096690

**BLUE
DRAGON**

Reprints: *The Inside View of Enforcement in China – Interview with Shen Rengan* first appeared in Managing Intellectual Property, July/August 2004, and is reprinted with kind permission.

Patent Litigation Takes Dramatic Step Forward – Interview with Cheng Yongshun first appeared in Managing Intellectual Property, China IP Focus , pp 15-18, and is reprinted with kind permission.

Rules of Engagement for IP Litigation appeared in Managing Intellectual Property May 2003. The interview is copyright Deacons Hong Kong and is reprinted with kind permission of Deacons.

www.bluedragon.com.hk

Catalogue details:
[Sun, C, Xue, V, *Insider's View: Dialogues on Intellectual Property in China*, (1st Ed, Blue Dragon, 2010) Softback 152 pp.]

Currency:
Based on materials available to the author as of 7 October 2010.

Disclaimer:
This work represents the opinion of the author at the time of writing and is not a substitute for professional legal advice.

ISBN 978-988-18250-6-3
BDA201006
Printed in Hong Kong

Foreword

By Professor Chen Meizhang

One of the key drivers of this book, Catherine Sun, has been my student for decades. I got to know her when she was a second-year law student of Peking University while I was teaching Intellectual Property (IP) Law there. At the time, she was very interested in IP and also passionate in promoting the development of IP domestically and internationally. The other key member Victor Xue was also my student (Class '77) when I was still a full time professor of Physics Department of Peking University. Victor is a scholar and author and has had many publications related to IP. After studying and living in the US for over a decade, he told me he would like to do something for the IP development in China. Then I introduced him to Catherine. In May 2007, Catherine who just started the Shanghai office of Foley & Lardner LLP, came to see me with Victor with this idea to publish an English report of IP minds in China. They planned to interview the policy makers, academic, judiciary and other players in the field, to provide an overview of the current status of China IP development. I fully supported it.

As the former Director of Peking University IP Teaching and Research Center and professor of law at the University, I quickly introduced the duo to several friends of mine whom Catherine also had known for years, to discuss the idea. Before summer in 2007, I organized a dinner for Catherine and Victor near Beida at Quan Ju De restaurant, several of my good friends came, including Duan Ruichun, Shen Rengan, Tian Lipu, Harold Wegner of George Washington University for a personal gathering. We all thought it was a good idea to build a bridge between China and the world by obtaining first-hand materials. From then on, I knew Victor and Catherine were starting to work on the project. I personally also accepted their interview to express my views on IP education in China. They interviewed government officials, judges and formal judges, professors and business leaders.

I am very pleased to write this Foreword to congratulate them upon completion of this project. I know both students are very busy in their lives and professional pursuit, but they managed a good team to have this project done in three years. I know this report will enable more foreign friends to understand what has been done in China in terms of IP protection and the efforts people in China have put on for the past

20-30 years. Through the effort of Chinese people, China has established an IP system and continued to improve it. China has been rapidly catching up in terms of IP protection, commercialization, management and strategy. I hope these two outstanding students could candidly introduce the current China IP system to our foreign friends, to better communicate and further understand each other, which would also benefit the implementation of the National IP Strategy; also continue their effort to update the report from time to time, so that the dialogue will be open to the outside world.

As an IP professor, I am very proud that two of my special students are making this significant contribution to the field. I will continue to lend whatever support they needed in this pursuit.

Professor Chen Meizhang

Late September 2010, in Beijing

Acknowledgement

As an IP practitioner in both US and China for the past twenty years or so, I have a strong feeling that communications on IP between the two countries are not at all reciprocal. There are a lot more English speaking Chinese who are language and culturally capable of understanding the US system, while there are very few Chinese speaking Americans who can read through the first hand development of the Chinese system. This has prompted this project – to discover what lies inside the minds of the key decision makers influencing Chinese IP system and then communicate the thoughts to the outside world so to facilitate mutual understanding and cooperation.

I would like to thank my partner Victor Xue who started the idea of doing this project in 2007 and also lent his support from so many angles in getting the project off the ground. During the three-year ordeal, we have received enormous support from so many people. In a non-exhaustive list, I would like to thank Professor Chen Meizhang, Mr. Duan Ruichun, Mr. Tian Lipu, Mr. Shen Rengan, Ms. Wen Xikai, Mr. Cheng Yongshun, Judge Kong Xiangju, Ms. Yang Yexuan, Professor Harold Wegner, Mr. Zhang Guangliang, as well as all the people who accepted our interviews. I must also thank our forever friend Late Judge Xu Jianchu, who passed away in 2009-now our interview to him reads exceptionally sad, memorable and valuable. We miss you, Judge Xu.

From the working team, I would like to thank Jo Wen Xu, Leo He, Vanessa Xu, Max Lin, Xiaoli Ren, and Sally Shen who have contributed a great deal in different ways to the completion of the project. Great team work!

I have to reemphasize that our interviewees come from a very diversified background representing the senior positions of his or her industry or profession in China. The opinions, statements and remarks expressed in their interviews do not represent the official positions of the professions, industries, organizations or entities they are in.

Further, as most interviews were conducted in Chinese, due to some of the message being lost in translation, the editors take full responsibility for any inaccuracies, omissions or misstatements.

I am so relieved now. It was a lot of hard work.

Catherine Sun

1 October, 2010

Acknowledgement

China is traveling in the fast lane, as we have witnessed her economical development over the last 30 years. Along with her growing economical power in the world, China's IPR issues and conflicts were also developed into a hot topic today. From professional IP practitioners to main stream business people to the media, the world have formulated different opinions and interpretations about law and enforcement in China.

I was fortunate to meet Mr. Duan Ruichun in 2006, who is one of the top Intellectual Properties experts in Chinese Government. From meetings with Mr. Duan and his colleagues in discussing Chinese IP law and enforcement, I noticed that the outside world was not fully aware of many of the developments in China. Many "mainstream" opinions about China were actually outdated. This is understandable because the pace of change is fast as China is trying to catch up 200 years of traveled path by Americans.

In 2007, I was accompanying a group of Chinese judges visiting a large US company headquartered in the Silicon Valley with a large branch in China. While in discussing IP protection issues in China, I noticed that legal professionals in the company interpret Chinese laws quite differently than the Chinese judges. The reason was the company obtained their knowledge about Chinese IP law indirectly which may include non-accurate opinions. This event triggered me to think of this project – to have first hand information from Chinese government officials and judges on their thoughts on IPR law and enforcement, serve as a bridge to shorten the distance between China and the world.

I am very fortunate to be able to partner with Catherine Sun in this project. As a top IP practitioner in both US and China, Catherine allocated significant portion of time from her busy schedule, utilized her resources in China, turned an "idea" into a project. Without her tireless efforts and constant encouragement, we would not be able to finish this project.

We are grateful to our teacher, Prof. Chen Meizhang of Peking University. With her generous help and support, we were able to get connected with several top government officials in charge of IP, such as SIPO Head Mr. Tian Lipu, former Director of NIPSO Professor Wen

Xikai and Mr. Shen Rengan, former Commissioner of Chinese Copyright Administration.

We are very grateful to those who accepted our interviews, especially to late Judge Xu Chujian who granted our interview just a few weeks after his cancer operation. In addition, I would also want to thank the following people for their support, opinion and encouragement for this project:

Judge Chen Jinchuan from Beijing High Court, Judge Dong Jianzhong from Beijing Intermediate Court, Judge Fang Shuangfu from Zhejiang High Court, Judge Tao Kaiyuan from Guangdong High Court, Judge Xie De-an from Henan High Court, Judge Lu Wende from Shanghai Middle Court, Ms. Zhao Huiling from National Copyright Administration, Mr. Chen Guangjun from National People's Congress, Mr. Ma Enzhong from National IPR Protection Group, Mr. Sun Yongjian, Mr. Zhang Xiaoyuan, Mr. Feng Chujian from Ministry of Science and Technology, Mr. Zhang Qin from SIPO, Mr. Zhou Siping from Trademark Appeals Board, State Administration of Industrial and Commerce, Professor Hal Wegner and Jo Xu of Foley-Lardner.

Victor Xue

30 September, 2010

Contents

PART ONE

THE INTERVIEWS

Professor Chen Meizhang

Time and Place:	Beijing Summer 2007
Attendees:	Victor Xue, IP author and scholar Wen Xu, currently a law student of Northwestern University Law School Prof. Chen Meizhang, a professor of IP College of Peking University

Professor Chen is the director of Teaching and Research Center of Intellectual Property at Peking University, Director of Patent Agency as well as a member of the Board of Directors, Intellectual Property Institute, Peking University. She has over 40 years teaching experience with half of them related to the education of Intellectual Property. She was appointed as Senior Research Fellow in Intellectual Property by the American Asia-Pacific Legal Institute in 1996.

Professor Chen headed or participated in ten research projects on intellectual property in the past 20 years, two of which won national awards for excellence. She has over 10 books and translated books and over 80 journal articles. She has also been invited to participate in international conferences or deliver lectures in the United States, Europe, Japan, Korea, Taipei and Hong Kong.

Her Distinguished Professional Affiliations include:

1. *Executive Director, Chinese Intellectual Property Research Institute*
2. *Member of the Board of Directors, Chinese Copyright Society*
3. *Consultant, Expert Consultancy Group of the Trademark Evaluation and Examination Committee, National Administration of Industry and Commerce*
4. *Consultant on Intellectual Property to the People's Courts in Beijing*
5. *Member of the Editing Committee of Intellectual Property and Science, Technology and Law magazines*
6. *Consultant of the Electronics and Intellectual Property magazine.*

Professor Chen Meizhang was one of the leading patent scholars in China. She was one of the founding members of the IP College of Peking University in early 1990s and has taught thousands of law students during her tenor at the Peking University. Below interview was originally conducted in Chinese and the English translation was unedited from the original interview. Professor Chen advised that we could cite her published articles regarding Chinese IP education.

Victor Xue: Prof. Chen could you talk about the influence of foreign education on China IP field, from the perspective of practitioner ratio in comparison of Western returnees with domestically trained professionals?

Prof. Chen: *With the globalization, the concept of overseas education underwent a big change over the past 20 years. The overseas educated students, in the early days, represented those outstanding undergraduate students, who graduated from Chinese top universities and continued the education abroad. However, various opportunities are available for most students to be educated overseas nowadays. The capability and quality of such overseas students differ,- some of them are even hard to find an appropriate job and therefore become seaweed so called "hai dai" (jobless). Those kinds of overseas students are not in the range of our discussion today. In the early 1980s, some of my students went abroad to continue their education and a lot of them made remarkable contribution in their own field. As a matter of fact, the conditions for research and development were far better overseas in particular in the 1980s. But over the past years with China's strong economic performance, the situation has been changing. We are glad to see that the scientific research capacity in China has a significant improvement during the past 20 years and more and more overseas students are returning to continue their careers in China. So we have seen more and more overseas returnees in all sorts of fields, including IP.*

Victor Xue: How are IP professionals educated in China?

Prof. Chen: *Citing her article: In the early 1980s, before the promulgation of Chinese Patent Law, the State Patent Office and the former State Education Commission organized nine training classes and trained the first batch of about 300 Chinese patent* *professionals. About 30 of them were selected and were sponsored to be educated overseas. Now, most of those professionals are the leaders in IP education field, IP academic research field, and IP practices field. In the mid of 1980s, the People's University of China established an IP education center and provided the double degree programs on IP law. Then, the center provided various IP education programs to various professionals, including doctor programs, master programs and double degree programs. The Peking University established its IP education center in 1985 and hosted a WIPO project in 1986. In 1993, the IP College was established in the Peking University and formally began to provide double degree program, master program and doctor program focusing on IP laws. Subsequently, Shanghai University, China Eastern University of Science and Technology and other universities (totally 10 universities) started their own IP programs. IP education developed rapidly at the university level.*

Victor Xue: Then how can we keep talent in China?

Prof. Chen: *The economic engine has driving China in a fast pace of development for the past thirty years. The fact that China has become one of the largest economic powers has created more opportunities for talents which serves to attract overseas talents as well. Structurally in academic field, we have a Changjiang Professorship Program in China and the recognized professionals in the program are paid at RMB 100,000 per year. The amount of money is not a lot but it can certainly retain some professionals-the economic value for this program apparently is trumped by the honorary value to a lot of the professionals who choose to stay. I have further noted that domestic professionals do not have very strong IP consciousness, therefore, the ownership of the research result is sometimes troublesome. From a positive perspective of view, we are glad to witness that such a problem has been attended to and the professionals' IP awareness has becoming stronger and stronger. The IP environment is also important to keep talents in China, in particular talents in scientific field.*

Victor Xue: What are the disadvantages of IP education system in China?

14

Prof. Chen: <u>*Citing her article*</u>*: Plenty of problems still exist in the Chinese IP education system. First, we did not educate enough IP professionals. Statistically, about 3,000 professionals were educated and trained in the IP filed from 1993 to 2005, and the average number was only around two hundred per year. Second, China's IP professional education system is not well structured, and undergraduates and double-degree graduates are short for demand. Third, the college education of basic IP knowledge is not well attended, therefore, relevant scholars and researchers lack sufficient IP awareness. Finally, the universities in China do not have enough teaching resources on IP.*

Victor Xue: From your point of view, are there any obvious differences of your students after they return from overseas?

Prof. Chen: *Let's take Catherine Sun as an example. She is an outstanding talent both before and after her overseas education. First, I think after she was educated and worked overseas for about ten years, she broadened her views and accumulated experience and had a global perspective on IP issues. Second, she understands the Chinese society and relevant legal environment in China due to her education and work here before she went overseas. Third , her oral and written English after all these years have become sufficiently well enough to enable her comprehensively understand foreign laws, rules and cases. Fourth, she is more familiar with international rules, and understands certain international practical issues comparatively. In sum, Catherine has become a balanced international talent after her overseas education and working experience.*

I think a lot of my students have had similar experience and growth like what Catherine had after they went abroad. In one of my education projects done for the Ministry of Education regarding how to make IP talents in China, I had Catherine's story as an example of what it takes to produce an international IP talent. It takes almost 15-20 years of hard work and millions of dollars to get there therefore the scale of that level wouldn't be big in a short period of time. But in my project, I also pointed out other programs that can provide more "mass" market IP talents in China such as the double degree program.

Victor Xue:	Can you briefly discuss the double degree IP program of Peking University?

Prof. Chen: *The IP double degree program of Peking University was launched in 1993, and we only recruited students from Peking University for the first three years (93-96). The students of those three years were very good and most of them are now holding the key positions of government, law firms, corporate IP departments, and patent firms in China. After that, we started to accept applications of students from other universities. Although the students were not as good as those of first three years, we still trained a great number of IP professionals and facilitated China's IP development very well. Recently, the enrolment of students for Master of Law is rising which has very high fees and tuitions but relatively lower admission standard, which negatively influences the development of IP double degree program. I'm concerned of the situation.*

[Editor Note: The double degree IP program of Peking University stopped for some years. After meeting Professor Chen and the Associate Dean of Peking University Law School on September 30th, 2010, we were gladly informed that the admission of double degree IP students renewed in fall term of 2010].

Victor Xue:	Could you tell us whether it is good for a student to continue the overseas education right after the undergraduate education or to work for a while before the overseas education?

Prof. Chen: *I think it depends on the individuals. The key is whether the continuity of the education is more important to the individual, or the explicit purpose of the overseas education is more important to the individual. I have seen students who continued the overseas education right after graduation, and I have also seen students who went abroad after working in China for several years. Both are doing well.*

Victor Xue:	In the IP field, what is the difference between the career development between the individuals who have science

> and engineering background and the individuals whose undergraduate education is law?

Prof. Chen: *The advantage of the individuals who have a bachelor of law degree is that they have better language skills and have a better understanding of the law. However, since they do not have technical background, sometimes it will be hard for them to conduct certain patent work. The individuals who have science or engineering background only may not have a solid legal background, but their legal knowledge can be accumulated and strengthened through work. Right now, more and more students who have both technical and legal education are focusing on IP, such as the double degree IP students. In my opinion, the individuals who have a technical background may carry further in patent work.*

> **Victor Xue:** What is your recommendation for establishing a good IP education and training system in China?

Prof. Chen: *Talents are the key to China IP system. I believe we should first focus on IP education in order to fundamentally improve China's IP protection situation. We should establish a comprehensive IP education and professional training system with China characteristics which should include the following five components: (1) Initial IP education in primary school; (2) Basic IP education in middle schools and high schools; (3) Required IP education in universities; (4) Professional IP education and training in universities, for the undergraduates, double degrees, postgraduates and doctors; and (5) IP training on the job who have a need of certain IP knowledge such as those who work for the government IP agencies, IP judges, lawyers and in house lawyers.*

Once we establish an integral IP education and training system, implement a reasonable national IP education strategy, set up enough IP training centers and offer sufficient IP programs in colleges and universities, and provide training programs to IP teaching resources, we will be able to significantly improve the IP education in China.

Ruichun Duan

Time and Place:	7 pm, August 28, 2007 @ SASAC Building (State-owned Assets Supervision and Administration Commission of the State Council) in Beijing
Attendees:	Mr. Youjian Sun, Ministry of Science and Technology Prof. Meizhang Chen, IP Center of Peking University Catherine Sun, Managing Partner, Foley & Lardner LLP Shanghai Office Victor Xue, IP author and scholar Harold Wegner, Professor, George Washington University Law School Wen Xu, currently a law student of Northwestern University Law School

Ruichun Duan is a senior cadre at ministerial level, a well-known expert in the field of Science & Technology as well as in economy and intellectual property. He had rich experiences in the area of enterprise technology renovation. He used to be the chief of Policies & Regulations and System Reform Department under Ministry of Science & Technology, during when he moderated the draft of a number of important laws, namely " Technology Contract Law", "Law on Science and Technology Progress".

He was the director of Intellectual Property Office under State Council during 1994 to 1998. He played a significant role in China's Intellectual Property Legislation and made great contribution to China's entry to World Trade Organization. He was a chief representative in the negotiation of China's Science &Technology Intellectual Property Cooperation with the US, the EU, and Russia. He was also a leading representative in WTO entry related Sino-American IP negotiation.

He joined the CCPCC Enterprise Committee from 2000, and worked as the Chairman of Supervisory Committee for Big State Owned Enterprises. After the organization structure reform in 2003, he resumed his role as the Chairman of Supervisory Board under SASAC (State-owned Assets

Supervision and Administration Commission). In 2007 he was in charge of the review of "National Intellectual Property Strategy Report". At present, he is a part-time professor in Peking University, Tsinghua University, China University of Mining and Technology and China National Defense University. He is the president of China Scientific and Technologic Laws Society, vice president of AIPPI (International Association for the Protection of Intellectual Property) China Sector.

Mr. Duan is one of the pioneers in making China's IP policy. He has participated a number of important trade and IP negotiations between China and other nations. Mr. Duan also teaches at various leading universities. Mr. Duan worked as the director of Intellectual Property Office under the State Council during 1994-1998, he played an important role in the design and organization of action plan to deter IP infringement. During 2000 to 2006, Mr. Duan worked as the Chairman of SASAC (State Owned Assets Supervision and Administration Commission), he paid special attention to the management and protection of enterprises IP portfolio. After his retirement from the minister role at SASAC, he currently holds the positions as the Director of China Science and Technology Law Society and the Executive Director of the China Advertisers Association.

Below interview was based on casual dinner conversation (therefore was not in a Q&A format) and shall not represent any official positions of the agencies or organizations Mr. Duan serves or has served.

During the banquet, Chairman Duan introduced the State-owned Assets Supervision and Administration Commission of the State Council (SASAC) and the supervisory Board to us. The SASAC manages over 140 big state-owned enterprises which are China's most important assets. The government dispatches supervisors to each enterprise to supervise the operation and management of the state-owned assets.

Chairman Duan encouraged big Chinese enterprises to build up their brands. There are 23 Chinese enterprises on Forbes Fortune 500 List, but none of them were included on Brand 100 list. Branding strategy is of great importance to big Chinese enterprises to establish better fame throughout the world. Your IP Interview project is helpful to introduce China's practice to U.S. I'm honored to be involved as a delegate of the first generation IP officials and experts in China.

Duan: *Last year I was invited to give a presentation to UC Berkeley University about the deficiency of China's IPR. I was not* *prepared for this topic, instead I talked about recent progress of China's IPR. In the end I addressed three weaknesses with China's current IP situation:*

First, infringement and piracy are still serious in China; second, abuse of IP rights is becoming a big issue; last, independent development of China's IP rights is at a very slow speed. I told the Berkeley audience that the last issue is the biggest obstacle to China's developing into an enduring innovative country. Without our own IPR, we are killing our creativity, which is the most destructive to China's development. We do need a number of creative enterprises with both R&D capability and strong IP portfolio.

The strategy and framework of China's IPR should not only be regarded as an outcome under the pressure of western world for their IPR protection in China but a necessary weapon for China to win in international competition as well.

Infringement and piracy in China shall be addressed seriously.

Infringement and piracy are not only the problems with China, but an international issue as well. With the rise of IP value in international trade regime, infringement has become more than a legal problem. According to some US reports, the damages caused by US domestic infringement is much more than those caused by other countries. The same is true for China: infringement is damaging China's future strategy and long term interest which is far more serious than economic loss. It is important to establish a long and sustained system to regulate serious IP infringement and crime effectively.

Abusing IP rights is becoming a big issue.

Same issue exists in IP protection system as in other legal systems, that is the proper reallocation of rights. It is important to balance the interests of property rights owner and that of the public society. Some IP rights owners abuse their right by accusing others, describing others as infringers in the media, filing complaints to the authorities and even taking malicious court actions without lawful foundation. Such abuse can also be found in some overseas companies. Some senior executives of multi-national companies do not follow normal legal procedures. They flew to China to meet our senior leaders in order to press their cases which are pending. This is a waste of our leaders' time and further it does not help the growth and development of China IP system through such uncommon "back door" approach. Abusing IP rights not only brings negative effect on normal IP protection system but also violates the interests of the public and distorts the market rules of competition.

China's independent IPR develops at a slow speed.

China is attracting more and more multi-national companies and foreign investments who mainly rely on advanced technologies and IP management. As a late comer, China's independent IPR is developing at a slow speed. The large amount of imported high technology coupled with lack of creativity will get in the way of Chinese enterprises' success in international competition. We encourage local Chinese companies to pay more attention to IP strategies, especially to brand strategies which do not need much technology and capital investment compared to patents.

Chairman Duan Recalling the old tough days.

As pioneers in Chinese IP field, Prof. Chen and Chairman Duan recalled their old days when they experienced the IP development for the past decades and IP education for three generations. In the past, Chinese IP experts could only listen to experts from other countries to talk about IP in international conferences or seminars, but now, the younger IP generation can debate with foreign experts on IP issues in international arena. They have strong confidence in China's IP development.

Problems with China's IP system.

There are four IP authorities in China. SIPO is in charge of patent, NCA (National Copyright Administration) is in charge of copyright matters, Trademark Office under State Agency for Industry and Commerce (SAIC) is in charge of trademark registration and protection; Customs is in charge of general IP borders protection. The four organizations operate independently and handle IP management without coordination. There once was a chance to allocate trademark office to SIPO but the plan was not carried out for certain historical reasons. It is not easy to combine these organizations into one at this moment. That is why it takes three years for a trademark to be registered. Over 100 trademark examiners under trademark office are supposed to inspect thousands of trademark applications, invalidations and dispute cases in a year. It is the reality and cannot be resolved in a short period.

No one can order how economy should react.

Chairman Duan pointed out that the development of IPR shall fit into economic condition. It was a big challenge to balance the interests of different countries in the negotiation for China's entry into WTO. According to WTO regulation, developing countries can start to protect patents in chemical pharmacy field after Year 2000 (the requirements for developed countries is 1986). The US negotiators required China to protect their patents in chemical pharmacy granted since 1976 but China only agreed to protect those granted since 1993.

It was humiliating for a country to be forced to accept retroactive protection. After deliberate consideration and balance of interests, a consensus was reached where China will provide 7-year's interim protection for patents of Sino-US joint ventures acquired before 1993, together with administrative enforcement. Through years of negotiation, China established our own IP framework according to WTO requirement but the process was very difficult.

Patent Implementation rate is not the only benchmark.

Patent implementation rate – usage rate of patented technology – was regarded as an important benchmark to determine whether a patent is good or bad. Actually it does not make much sense. In Japan many patents were registered not for usage but for defensive protection and strategic reasons. It is strange to require each patent to be implemented in IP system. Our top level IP officials should be cautious in the guidance to Chinese enterprises to avoid any confusion.

Chairman Duan told us several stories about China's WTO IP negotiation. IP interests is public interests which we shall not give up easily. Sometimes political decisions may affect public interests but the negotiators including Madam Wu Yi have tried their best to protect China's public interests.

Chairman Duan mentioned a tactic employed by some big foreign companies: they would contact senior leaders in China directly. For instance, the CEO of a big US company would invite Vice Premier or other senior government officials to dinner and talk about specific IP issues. This tactic worked well in the past. However, Chairman Duan thinks it is not a correct approach to deal with IP issue, by involving senior leaders, as the company bypasses normal proceedings for complaints and suggestion of IP system. It leads to the chaos of IP workflow and is a waste of a leader's valuable time.

Foreign exchange programs.

Chairman Duan was very supportive for senior Chinese officials and judges to participate in exchange programs with Berkeley University. It's important for our judges and officials to have exposure to foreign ways of thinking. Some of us in China are well aware of international developments in IP area. But most judges are still lack of such knowledge. The group sent to Berkeley was very senior, they went there not just to learn but also to exchange ideas. As the most influential figures in China, it was impossible for those judges and officials to switch their thinking into US style, while it was important for them to communicate and build up relationship.

Were the expectations of the several US corporate sponsors to the Berkeley program met?

The sponsorship does help to speed up the progress and most sponsors are willing to help facilitate communications between China and US. Those Chinese officials were very senior, it was not easy for them to leave their posts for three weeks, Chinese government also made great contributions to this program. However a few sponsors had unreasonable expectation-they wished to obtain favors from Chinese judges, some even tried to invite ("bribe") our judges. These companies were indeed naive. They probably did not understand the most important thing for Chinese judges and government officials are their career path, they always try to avoid the accusation of being brainwashed by the western world. They will try to prove that they are NOT influenced. One judge attending the program expressed that he would be more cautious when dealing with US affairs in the future. He may even be unfavorable to the US companies to show he is not biased. It may disappoint those sponsors with expectations to gain immediate favors.

****

Chairman Duan continued to be approachable after the dinner in summer 2007. On June 19th, 2009, in an international comparative IP conference moderated by Catherine Sun in Beijing, Chairman Duan delivered a key note speech entitled "Brand, An Integrated Intellectual Property". He outlined following strategies for Chinese enterprises to deal with IP risks in international competition:

- Transform from made in China to innovate in China
- Transform from IP deprived to IP rich
- Understand the rules of the game
- Switch from fight solo to industry alliance
- Improve enterprises' soft power-grasp rules of the games, and promote strategies for IP, standards, and brands.

At the end of his presentation, Chairman Duan concluded that the financial crisis has changed the climate of world economy, but it did not change the rules of innovation. Science and technology still determines the productivity which has not been changed but will play an increasingly important role. The worldwide battle between R&D of IP before commercialization, and branding management after commercialization, will be more fierce. Innovation will be the engine to drive economy out of recession. In China, innovation shall not stop at technology commercialization. We should nurture more world leading brands as they represent integrated intellectual property including new technology, management, sales and so on. Technology has no national boundary, but brands have. These future created competitive international brands will become the national treasures, pride of Chinese People, and vehicles to achieve maximum profits.

Shen Rengan

The inside view of enforcement in China

Foreign companies know that copyright infringement in China is rife. But as Shen Rengan, deputy commissioner of the National Copyright Administration of China, explains , the country's copyright law offers them a number of avenues for enforcing their rights. Interview by **Catherine Sun.**

Shen Rengan is the Deputy Commissioner of the National Copyright Administration of China, the body that implements the country's copyright laws. The NCAC was set up in 1985 directly under the control of the State Council of China. It also investigates cases of copyright infringement deemed to affect the public interest and is in charge of approving bodies that deal with collective administration of copyright, foreign-related copyright agencies and copyright arbitration agencies. Shen Rengan is in charge of legal affairs at the NCAC, which he joined in 1985. He was deputy head of the group that drafted China's Copyright Law, which came into force in June 1991 and has been vice-chair of WIPO's standing committee on copyright

Ms. Sun:	What does China plan to do to enforce copyright protection as part of its recent commitments to strengthen IP rights?

Shen: *Administrative enforcement is a unique feature that China has used for some time to strengthen IP enforcement. The NCAC amended the Implementing Measures of Copyright Administrative Sanction in the summer of 2003. These measures took effect on September 1 2003. The NCAC and its local bureaux may now initiate enforcement actions on their own or launch an action after receiving a complaint from a copyright owner. As a matter of practice, when we initiate actions we normally combine forces with other agencies such as the local police, local offices of the Administration for Industry and Commerce (AIC), Customs, the cultural authorities and administration offices in charge of press and publications. We think combined actions strengthen market supervision and administration. We will continue to take these combined actions.*

Ms. Sun:	How do copyright authorities identify a target before they take administrative action?

Shen: *Copyright administrative authorities use channels such as report hotlines, market surveillance and reports from rights holders or interested parties for obtaining information. We share information with other agencies before we take any combined actions.*

Ms. Sun:	If a complaint is received from a copyright owner or holder, what are the threshold requirements before the copyright authorities decide to accept the case?

Shen: *Article 47 of the revised Chinese Copyright Law requires that the infringing activities alleged in the complaint must be serious enough that they also harm the so-called public interest before a copyright administrative enforcement action can be taken. The complainant must demonstrate that the public interest has been injured, not just that the complainant's own commercial interests have been injured.*

Ms. Sun:	Was there a requirement that the public interest be injured before the Copyright Law was revised on 27 October 2001?

Shen: *The old Copyright Law did not specify this, but in practice the copyright authorities did actually require this element to be demonstrated.*

Ms. Sun:	How can a foreign company start a copyright administrative enforcement action?

Shen: *A foreign company must first have a definitive target and evidence that supports their allegation of infringement. They can then petition the local copyright authority that is located at the place of infringement, or which otherwise has jurisdiction.*

Ms. Sun:	Can a foreign company initiate a copyright administrative enforcement action at the central level?

Shen: *Article 37 of the Copyright Implementing Rules allows a rights holder, including a foreign company, to petition a case that has nationwide impact to the NCAC. Local copyright authorities adjudicate other cases.*

Under the Implementing Measures of Copyright Administrative Sanction, a copyright authority at a higher level may choose to adjudicate cases with significant impact even though a copyright authority at a lower level has jurisdiction. Similarly, a copyright authority at a lower level may transfer a significant and complex case to a higher level authority.

Ms. Sun: Do copyright administrative authorities transfer cases to other agencies?

Shen: *If a case does not fall within the scope of the copyright law, the copyright administrative authorities will transfer the case to an agency with jurisdiction, such as the AIC or the administrative authorities in charge of patents. If the alleged infringement is subject to criminal liability, the copyright administrative authorities will transfer the case to the relevant criminal court or to the public prosecutors.*

Ms. Sun: How often do copyright administrative authorities collect evidence when they receive requests from complainants? What burden of proof must the applicant satisfy before the authorities will collect evidence?

Shen: *The copyright administrative authorities have two ways of obtaining evidence: one is to require the complainant to produce evidence to support their claims. Of course, the authorities will verify the submitted evidence. The other way is for us to conduct our own investigations to collect evidence if such an action is warranted.*

Ms. Sun: Can you explain what happens after a complainant initiates a copyright administrative enforcement action?

Shen: *The Implementing Measures of Copyright Administrative Sanction require a rights holder to submit a written complaint to start the process. The copyright administrative authorities must decide whether to accept the case within 15* *days of receiving a complaint. In doing so, they have to consider whether a complaint falls within the scope of Article 47 of the revised Copyright Law. If the copyright administrative authorities believe the case should not be accepted, we notify the complainant in writing. If we accept it, there are several stages to go through, including collecting evidence, investigating and hearing the case, and rendering and enforcing the decision. There is no statutory deadline as to how quickly we must render a decision. The time it takes us to conclude a case pretty much depends on its complexity.*

Ms. Sun:	How easy is it to enforce a decision rendered by the copyright administrative authorities?

Shen: *We think it is easy. We seldom experience problems in enforcing our decisions.*

Ms. Sun:	What is the procedure to get a review of a copyright administrative decision?

Shen: *The parties may seek review from an administrative authority at a higher level or from the legal department of the government at the same level. If a party is still not satisfied with the result, they may lodge an administrative lawsuit – but this only happens rarely.*

Ms. Sun:	What are the costs involved in a copyright administrative enforcement action?

Shen: *The copyright administrative authorities do not charge fees.*

Ms. Sun:	What is the evidential value of an administrative decision in a civil lawsuit?

Shen: *According to civil law procedures in China, the courts must examine the evidence and reach a decision independently.*

Ms. Sun:	How often do foreign companies take copyright administrative actions in China?

Shen: *Very rarely. Administrative enforcement mechanisms have been predominantly employed by Chinese copyright owners* *and holders. The main areas for copyright administrative actions focus on piracy of books, motion pictures, software, and applied arts.*

I guess the reason for there being so few copyright administrative actions brought by foreign companies is primarily that administrative actions are unique to China. The process is unfamiliar to foreign companies who are more comfortable with going to court to resolve copyright disputes. In addition, a complainant is required to establish that there has been injury to the public interest, which may discourage foreign companies from pursuing the matter. Finally, administrative actions cannot result in an award of damages and this may make them less attractive to foreign companies.

Ms. Sun:	Are copyright-related international treaties such as such as the Berne Convention, TRIPs, WCT and WPPT binding in China?

Shen: *Article 142 of the General Principles of Civil Law says that where the provisions of an international treaty which China has concluded or acceded to differ from the civil laws of China, the provisions of the international treaty shall prevail, with the exception of those articles to which China has made a reservation. This means that a qualified international treaty should have equal validity with a domestic law.*

Ms. Sun:	Can a foreign party sue for copyright infringement or bring an administrative action based purely upon an international treaty, such as the Berne Convention or TRIPs?

Shen: *No. They must cite a domestic law. According to the principles in the Berne Convention and other international treaties, a claim in a domestic member country must be decided in accordance with that country's domestic law.*

Ms. Sun:	The 2001 revised Copyright Law widened the scope of copyright infringement to encompass computer networks, the unauthorized rental of audio visual works, wilful sabotage of technological measures and so on. Yet the Chinese criminal code and its corresponding judicial interpretations have not been modified to

> criminalize these new types of infringement. Do you think additional copyright crimes will be added?

Shen: *We do not have much experience of these new types of digital copyright infringement and we are still at the stage of understanding these new forms of infringement – as are most countries in the world. Therefore, it might take some time to incorporate them into the Chinese criminal code.*

Ms. Sun: What is the status of copyright crime in China?

Shen: *China has been fighting piracy very hard by using various means including criminal mechanisms. The Standing Committee of National People's Congress issued provisions on punishing copyright crimes in 1994. The Criminal Code was amended in 1997 to include two copyright-related crimes. These provide for a maximum penalty of seven years imprisonment plus fines. The Supreme People's Court and Supreme People's Procuratorate have since issued corresponding judicial interpretations to strengthen criminal enforcement. Procedure-wise, a copyright crime can be prosecuted through public prosecution or by way of a private prosecution – which may include civil claims for damages. China's copyright criminal sanctions conform to Article 61 of TRIPs, which provides standards for criminal sanctions for commercial copyright piracy. There was a recent case in Fujian Province where the offender was sentenced to five years in prison and a fine of Rmb200,000 ($24,200). Statistics on copyright criminal cases are still incomplete because some cases may be treated as other economic crimes. China is in the process of making judicial interpretations that will lower the threshold requirement for IP criminal sanctions and specify more infringing activities.*

Ms. Sun: China has recently extended copyright infringement to the sabotaging of technological measures. Do you think this could make certain uncopyrightable materials copyrightable by putting technological measures over their digital format?

Shen: *The purpose of the technological measures should be to protect certain copyrightable materials by making it easier to establish infringement.*

Ms. Sun:	What is your view on copyright protection of applied arts for industrial use in China?

Shen: *The Chinese Copyright Law does not specify applied arts as a separate subject matter. Under the Berne Convention, applied arts may be protected for 25 years. But both domestic and foreign owners may consider protecting applied arts under the category of fine arts, which will enjoy longer-term protection such as the life of the author plus 50 years.*

Ms. Sun:	Are there any private collective copyright administration bodies in China?

Shen: *At the moment there is only the Music Copyright Society of China (MCSC). Other collective bodies in areas relating to, for instance, photographic works, literary works and audio-visual works are being established.*

Ms. Sun:	Can a foreign collective body establish a presence in China?

Shen: *Foreign collective bodies can only form agency relationships with a Chinese counterpart.*

Ms. Sun:	Is copyright registration mandatory in China?

Shen: *Before the new software copyright regulations took effect in 2002, it was only mandatory to register software copyright. Now, copyright registration for all forms of copyright works is voluntary. But registration shows prima facie ownership, which has significant evidentiary value in administrative actions and litigation. Even if a copyright is not registered, the rights holder can still bring an enforcement action if they provide evidence of ownership. A registration certificate may be the easiest way of proving prima facie ownership, which will shift the burden to the other side to prove otherwise.*

Article 47

The infringement activities specified in Article 47 apply to a party that:

- without authorization, reproduces, distributes, performs, shows, broadcasts, compiles or disseminates another's work via public networks, except as provided by the Copyright Law;
- publishes books in which exclusive publication rights belong to others;
- without the authorization of a performer, reproduces or distributes sound recordings of a performance, or publicly transmits the performance via information networks, except as provided by the Copyright Law;
- without authorization, broadcasts or reproduces radio and TV programmes, except as provided by the Copyright Law;
- without authorization of the copyright owner/holder, purposefully avoids or destroys the copyright protective measures attached to a work or sound recording product, except as provided by laws or administrative regulations;
- without authorization of the copyright owner/holder, purposefully deletes or modifies digital ownership management information of a work or a sound recording product, except as provided by laws or administrative regulations; and produces and/or sells a work that falsely asserts authorship.

Qing Huang

Time and Place:	10:30 am, August 29, 2007 at SIPO Building
Attendees:	Qing Huang, Secretary General of State IP Strategy Office Victor Xue, IP author and scholar Wen Xu, currently a law student of Northwestern University Law School

Huang Qing is Secretary General of State IP Strategy Office and Chief of Protection and Coordination Department under SIPO (State Intellectual Property Office of the PRC). He got his bachelor's degree from Wuxi Light Industry University, master's degree from Beijing University of Technology; he also studied industry property law, management and economy courses in WIPO Worldwide Academy. He entered SIPO in 1993 and has worked for Chemistry Review Department; Preliminary Examination Department, Patent Bureau and Informatization Office. He gained rich experiences and unique insight after spending many years in Patent Inspection, Preliminary Examination, Flow Management, Information Management, IP Strategy Planning and IP Protection.

Mr. Huang informed us that the conversation was private in nature between friends which should not be quoted to represent any official position. Below interview was originally conducted in Chinese and the English translation was unedited from the original interview.

Victor Xue:	What do you think is the nature of intellectual property rights?

Mr. Huang:	*Let me tell you a story first: a forest owner contracts his forest to a farmer with two options, – term of 5 years and 50 years. If the farmer only gets five years to manage the forest, to make the most profit he will probably cut down all trees, even the small ones which will eventually destroy the ecology; however if he is granted 50 years' rights, he will probably plant more trees, and carry on a long-term plan. This story shows it's a*

must for a nation to establish a proper intellectual property system in order to keep its economy grow prosperously. The establishment of a clear property rights system is essential to the transformation of high-tech achievements and will have deep impact on our mission to transfer from "Made in China" to "Innovated in China". I think there are mainly three reasons why the United States keeps emphasizing on China's IP issues. First, the pressure of RMB appreciation leads to the reduction of Sino-US trade surplus; Second, China's strict market accession makes it less possible for dominant US industries to earn high profit in China; Third, the US wishes to expand its profitable opportunities in China, such as access to service industry. Therefore the economic nature of IP issues results in the Western world not being satisfied no matter what China is doing in this regard, and the international IPR disputes will continue to exist for a very long period. Therefore, besides learning advanced IP experience and practice from the West, China shall follow our economic development rules and establish our own IPR system gradually rather than be anxious and simply borrow the western approaches.

Victor Xue: Why there is less action on counterfeiting from luxury goods segment?

Mr. Huang: *The luxury goods consumers do not overlap with those who purchase fake goods. The sales volume of fake goods, no matter big or small, will not affect the sales volume of authentic ones. Therefore without being driven by economic interests, no wonder the luxurious industry does not carry out much action on counterfeiting. Yet they still deal with counterfeiting in consideration of brand/image protection.*

Victor Xue: What's the relationship between IPR and economic development stage?

Mr. Huang: *The IPR development of Japan has also been through similar historical process, therefore I have strong confidence in the improvement of China's IPR level. However, by analyzing some domestic data related to intellectual property, you will* *find even if the numbers themselves are good ones, i.e. GDP, due to incapability of analyzing the data, how to utilize such data is often a problem in China. It's wrong to attach too much importance to pursuing data, yet we can't ignore the function of data as well.*

Victor Xue:	Some officials pointed out it's not a scientific statistics method to look at the rate of patent implementation, as it shows lack of understanding of intellectual property systems. What's your opinion?

Mr. Huang: *China used to adopt only one standard to measure patents, that is the quantity of patent application. Later, rate of patent implementation was taken into consideration. To be frank, such rate itself doesn't mean a lot, but when it is combined with the quantity of patent application, we get more comprehensive result. Multi-dimensional evaluation system is certainly more scientific than single-dimensional one.*

Victor Xue:	Do you think current IPR system will limit innovation and the progress of technology?

Mr. Huang: *As I mentioned earlier, the level of IPR development shall cater to the level of economic development. At present, we are still at elementary level of economic development, majority of our industries are low value-added, high consumptive of natural resources. On the other hand, IPR, patent in particular, requires considerable amount of accumulation, both in respect to capital and human resources. Many Chinese enterprises are trying hard to survive now, they may even die out in the process of accumulation. How can an enterprise pay attention to innovation and technology progress when it cannot even survive? Actually it's not conflicting. I believe enterprises will take the initiative to protect IPR when it grows to certain level. Take a look at coastal provinces, enterprises have stronger desire to seek protection of IPR than those in inland provinces. In Zhejiang Province, almost every company is trying to protect its trademark and design patent. When a company has conquered survival issues, they will spontaneously consider their future*

35

development. Many Chinese enterprises are aware that a company without IPR will not last long. For those who are not capable of IPR protection at present, this is more of a slogan than practice.

Mr. Huang: *According to my personal study, IP problems are more likely to occur to companies in the region between coastal region and inland region. In other words, most IP problems lie in the companies which desire to develop but not fully developed yet. I constantly think that advanced intellectual property concept can be planted in inland if we encourage developed coastal companies (especially. Those who target domestic market) to move to inland. The more and deeper such regional migration is, the better the achievement will be. Certainly there are practical issues to be considered such as transportation costs before the idea can be realized. More and more multinational companies will enter inland for sure, but due to the inconvenience of transportation, it still takes years to reduce high transportation costs.*

Victor Xue:	Mr. Huang further commented below issues during the interview

The essence of transfer of technology results lies in solving ownership issue.

Mr. Huang talked about the difficulties of transferring technology results in the universities and research institutes. It is basically resulted from a number of reasons: first, the award of innovation and invention offered by universities and research institutes is too high, technology personnel lives a happy life with the award so are now pressed to commercialize the technology; Second, cooperation cost is too high. Many interested parties drew back because of the high transaction cost caused by different expectations on technology valuation, confusion of procedures and unclear ownership rights. Third, ownership issue. The ownership of property rights of technology are often unclear. Take Lenovo for example, Lenovo borrowed 2 million RMB from Computer Research Center when it started the business, it's hard to separate the assets of the two organizations apart even now. Such unclear ownership rights system will have negative effect on the development of enterprises. The government is making many attempts to solve the problem in the hope that more research and science & technology achievements can be turned into industrial production.

The Intellectual Property policy should not change frequently.

Mr. Huang mentioned the forest case again. If the government decides to take back the right of use when it discovers some contractors cut down trees to gain short-term profit, such decision will not harm those who signed 5-years contract at all since they have got everything they wanted, on the contrary those who signed 50-year contract will be victims because they have just planted trees and expected for future growth. If the government does not keep a persistent policy, the short-sighted owners who only care about short term benefits will go from bad to worse, while those who hope for sustainable development will suffer greater loss. The government should sit back and work on policy guidance and reform and allow enough time for these policies to show their effects.

Brand creation is more important than technology innovation.

Mr. Huang: The government shall attach same importance to brand creation as to technology innovation. It is easier and cheaper to develop a brand than to create a patent, and a necessary step for future development. It usually takes 3-5 years for technology achievements to be commercialized if not longer, while to most companies, generating profit is much more important than creating patents. In comparison, brand creation requires less investment and more suitable to Chinese companies at current stage when Chinese enterprises have not reached overall technology innovation. When they become stronger in the future, they will safeguard their IP rights against foreign parties as well.

Research of China's IPR is short of economic experts.

Mr. Huang: IPR is an economic tool. One must find the key to economy in order to develop IPR system. The main problem with Chinese decision-makers is that we are short of generalists who are familiar with law, technology and economics at the same time. We have experts in law, we have experts in technology but we are short of experts in economy. A good policy is one that suits economic rules, suits economic development phase, that can lead China's IP development to a better direction.

Judge Kong Xiangjun

Time and Place:	August 28, 2007 2:00pm @ Supreme People's Court ("SPC"), Beijing
Attendees:	Catherine Sun, Managing Partner, Foley & Lardner LLP Shanghai Office Victor Xue, IP author and scholar Harold Wegner, Professor, George Washington University Law School Wen Xu, currently a law student of Northwestern University Law School

Honorable Kong Xiangjun is the Chief Judge of the Intellectual Property Tribunal of the Supreme People's Court of China. He was born in 1965 in Dingtao County, Shandong Province, coming from the Confucius Family of the 75th generation. He got Doctor's degree of Civil and Commercial Law from China University of Politics & Law and was a post doctorate in Renmin University. He was on the list of China 10 Distinguished Young Jurist in 2006 and on the Managing IP Magazine's annual list of 50 most influential people in IP in 2009. He is a leading scholar in the research area of unfair competition law, anti-monopoly law and intellectual property law in China. He published more than 200 academic works on corporation law, contract law, unfair competition law, anti-monopoly law, trade secret law, TRIPs, WTO law, and legal construction method, etc. Many of his works have been chosen as university textbooks for undergraduates and post graduates.

Judge Kong is the associate chief judge of IP tribunal of Supreme People's Court (SPC). Before the interview, Judge Kong showed the guests a tour around SPC buildings and courtrooms and introduced the SPC internal structure. Professor Wegner was impressed by a slogan posted inside the SPC building, "heavy as mountains, solid as rocks, bright as a mirror and transparent as water" ("重如山、牢如石、亮如镜、清如水"). We thanked Judge Kong to accept our interview and informed that the final neutral report will be published in English. Judge Kong commented that it was a meaningful program to collect interviews from persons in different positions, so the interviewees should frankly speak on their own practice areas based on their experience. We are aiming to truly report the current China IP situation to the foreign readers who are interested in China IP practice. The report may ease or clarify the misunderstanding of China IP practice understood and reported by foreign lawyers and foreign media.

Ms. Sun:	Sometimes foreign lawyers and media may be biased in reporting China IP. What do you think about these foreign reports?

Kong: *A lot of these foreign reporters are not familiar with the IP practice in China. On the contrary, we understand the foreign IP practice very well, particularly the US practice. As a front line judge, I need to know the current development and IP practice in the world, in order to improve my ability of adjudicating cases. A neutral report should not only talk about the concept but also the actual legal practice. To report undistorted facts is always the best way to describe the situation. No matter what the foreigners complain, our only goal is to enforce China IP laws equally and fairly.*

Ms. Sun:	Due to current insufficient monetary relief, we still have not seen important patents litigating in China, do you agree?

Kong: *Actually, several patent cases relating to certain key patents have been filed in front of the Court, such as **Founder vs. Blizzard**, in which case Founder claims one hundred million Yuan in damages. The Beijing High People's Court accepted the complaint in August. For the compensation calculation, U.S. court has a more complicated method than ours.*

[**Editorial Note:** within two years after the interview, we have seen a few high profile patent cases litigated in China such as *Chint vs. Schneider, Holley vs. Samsung*, and *Strix* case].

Ms. Sun:	How many cases does SPC handle annually?

Kong: *Each year, the SPC receives around 10 appeal cases and over 100 certiorari petitions. The IP Tribunal of SPC has 8 judges in total, but two of them are chief judges who do not have the duty to hear cases. Meanwhile, according to the training schedule of SPC, two of the remaining six judges need participate routine training programs on a rotating basis.*

Therefore, with limited manpower, the workload of each judge in IP Tribunal is quite heavy.

Ms. Sun: How do you handle the *certiorari* cases for retrial?

Kong: *For the retrial cases, the parties do not need to pay any court fees. We will focus on the review of the legal grounds and reasoning part of the judgment, sometimes as well as the facts. The procedure of retrial cases is of the same as appeal cases, so we accept new evidence during the retrial. However, the SPC does not review all cases petitioned certiorari for retrial.*

Ms. Sun: What else do you do apart from hearing the cases?

Kong: *We will also need to issue judicial interpretations from time to time. Sometimes, we need help the lower courts on addressing certain practical issues. Meetings, trainings and other administrative duties also take substantial of our working hours.*

Ms. Sun: How does the SPC's decision influence the lower courts' judgment?

Kong: *We are establishing a model case system to guide the lower courts' judgment. Specifically, SPC will select certain representative judgments for lower courts' guidance. The guiding judgments will have substantial influence on the lower courts' decision. If the lower court does not follow the guidance to decide a case, the case will probably be reversed by the higher court. Sometimes, the guiding cases might be deemed as an informal interpretation of the laws, instead of the judicial interpretations.*

Ms. Sun: How many trainings do you do for the judges of lower courts?

Kong: *Around six to seven times per year.*

Ms. Sun: How much time do you spend on adjudicating cases?

Kong: *It is hard to provide a precise answer. I spend plenty of time on thinking and understanding the law and regulations* *which is a crucial part to my job, because the judgment of SPC is not only a decision, but also serves as a guidance for the decisions of similar cases. I need consider the present law from a historic and philosophical perspective. Due to the fast development of IP cases, SPC is increasing the focus on the reasoning of IP case judgment.*

Ms. Sun:	How many judicial interpretations are published every year? What is the process?

Kong: *It is hard to calculate, because there is no limitation or task requirement. The process for issuing an interpretation is similar to the enactment of a law. The process includes establishment of the project, initial draft of the interpretation, internal discussion of the draft, open to public comments, finalization of the interpretation, then submission for judicial committee's approval and issuance. The whole process can be done within half a year or several years. It depends on actual contents and the demand of the interpretation.*

Wegner: *Japan and Germany are both code law countries, but the system does not ignore judges' opinion. The judges' opinion is treated as what "the God said", and such opinions are an important part in the statute law system.*

Ms. Sun:	How do the SPC's cases influence the lower courts?

Wegner: *Courts have an important role on the public's education. The law is stiff and complex, and the judges have the authority to decide a case by considering the different actual situations. Sometimes, judges need do the research to compare the laws in different jurisdictions in order to update their knowledge. Scholars' articles may also have certain influence on judges' decisions.*

Kong: *As far as I know, the judges in the lower courts will firstly refer to the similar cases decided by higher courts or peer courts, and then refer to the relevant judicial interpretations. The precedent cases are becoming more and more important nowadays. Due to the specific facts of each case, SPC's judgment can not be used as a template for all cases, but at least it can be referred to in similar cases. Such a judging template is really helpful for the lower courts' growth.*

41

Compared with American legal system, the judges of SPC rarely consider the scholars' opinions, because most of the opinions are unpractical or out of date. The SPC's judges consider the advanced legal theory and make their decision based on China's own situation. We have spent lots of time studying the foreign cases and the advanced legal theory. The China court system is open minded, but will never blindly follow the foreign practice.

Wegner: *The comparative law study is valuable, and we should encourage more investment on this. On one hand, we are very glad to read the Chinese judgment, if certain institutes or companies (e.g. Westlaw) can translate the Chinese judgment into English and make them accessible. On the other hand, the overseas law schools or research centers can be helpful on the comparative research in different jurisdictions, if the SPC would like to cooperate with them. The SPC can support such a comparative research program by translating the Chinese judgments and encouraging more professionals to study the laws of America, EU or other countries.*

Kong: *Due to the limited manpower, SPC is not able to work on the translation of the judgments. But certain companies and institutes have begun such a project or business, such as Chinalawinfo (www.Chinalawinfo.com), founded by Peking University.*

Ms. Sun: We are very interested in evidence rules in China. Would you please take about the discovery procedure in China?

Kong: *The Several Provisions regarding the Evidence in Civil Procedure issued in 2001 contains some discovery rules, therefore, Chinese legal system currently has basic rules for evidence discovery, evidence exchange and evidence questioning. China does not copy all America discovery rules, and our rules are not as complicated as America's. For example, China court does not have special court hearing to argue for evidence discovery. In my opinion, a complex evidence discovery procedure consumes too much time in litigation.*

Kong: *The fact admitted by one party can be confirmed, meanwhile the other party can question the evidence in an open court.*

We have the similar rules as the admission by parties in the America. As I mentioned before, we have the basic discovery rules, but do not entirely follow American procedures.

Ms. Sun:	If the discovery is insufficient, will the party perjuring or destroying evidence be punished?

Kong: *Of course. The above behaviors are serious, and we have detention, fines and criminal penalty to punish the persons engaging in such wrongful acts.*

Ms. Sun:	How long does SPC spend on hearing a case?

Kong: *Normally one day. The cases submitted to the SPC already have clear facts, therefore, the SPC judges do not need to spend too much time on the facts, but they will spend lots of time on the reasoning part of the judgment.*

We benefit from U.S. case law. Frankly speaking, US practice is more important to China than European practice, not only because US is one of the most important countries, but also due to more advanced legal technology developed by the Americans. We studied and absorbed the advanced American legal principles to draft Chinese judicial interpretations, and in consideration of China's own situation. However, due to the obscure language used by the judges, sometimes we have certain difficulties to understand the US judgment completely. Before making a decision, I study the latest cases and advanced achievements, in order to ensure my decision is accurate and in line with the global trend of IP development. As a judge, I have to resolve the practical problems by applying various legal theories, which is a tough and challenging job.

Ms. Sun:	How is the English skill of judges in SPC's IP tribunal?

Kong: *Their English skills are all better than mine. (Laugh) Many judges are educated overseas after becoming judges. From a judge's point of view, the English reading skill is most important. Some SPC judges can use English as their working language.*

Ms. Sun:	Would you please talk about doctrine of equivalent?

Kong: *We introduced the doctrine of equivalent into our patent law in 2001, when a debate on the principle between US IP Judges was still ongoing. Sometimes, our IP legal system is more advanced than yours.(Laugh)*

Ms. Sun:	What do you think of our program?

Kong: *The program is excellent and bears heavy responsibilities. It is not an easy task to make U.S. IP professionals understand China IP situation. I hope to be updated by emails and will be glad to receive additional questions. Different routes will lead you to the same destination (Judge Kong citing an old Chinese saying in conclusion).*

Judge
Cheng Yongshun

Time and Place:	March 3rd, 2009 Radission Sas Langsheng Hotel in Shanghai
Attendees:	Mr. Cheng Yongshun, Director of Beijing Intellectual Property Institute Ms. Wen Xu, Currently a law student of Northwestern University

Mr. Cheng began his IP career in January 1985. He is among the first judges to hear IP cases in China and has since presided over a great number of significant IP cases.

Mr. Cheng joined Beijing High People's Court in 1982 as an associate judge and became judge of the commercial division, deputy head of the Intellectual Property Division, then worked his way up to be head of the Industry Property Group of the IP division of the Supreme People's Court of China. He retired in March 2005 as a senior judge from the Beijing High People's Court.

Upon retiring from the Beijing High People's Court, Mr. Cheng established the Beijing Intellectual Property Institute, where he engaged in IP research and consultancy, doing research, training and counseling for both corporations and governments.

Titles & Affiliations

- *Administrative director of the China Intellectual Property Institute, the China Trademark Association and the Intellectual Property Institute of the China Law Society*
- *Depute secretary-general and administrative director of China Science and Technology Law Institute*
- *Director of the China Copyright Association*
- *Advisor to the Trademark Review and Adjudication Board of the State Administration of Industry and Commerce*

- *Member of the Legal Committee of the China Advertising Association*
- *Panel Member of the Domain Name Disputes Resolution Center, China Patent Protection Association*
- *Member of the Professoriate of the Tsinghua University Professional Manager Training Center*

Publications
- *Editor-in-chief, Questions and Answers for Technology Contract Litigation, Beijing Science & Technology Press, 1990.*
- *Author, Patent Litigation, Patent Publication Press, 1993.*
- *Author, Research on Hot and Hard Issues of Industry Property, People's Court Press, 1996.*
- *Editor-in-chief, Judicial Review of Patent Cases 1988-1998, Patent Publication Press, 1999.*
- *Editor-in-chief, Judicial Review of Patent Cases 1994-2001, Intellectual Property Press, 2003.*
- *Editor-in-chief, Practice of Patent Infringement Establishment, Law Press, 2002.*
- *Editor-in-chief, Patent Administrative Litigation Practice, Law Press, 2003.*
- *Editor-in-chief, Court Decisions of Intellectual Property (1-5), Science Press, 2003.*
- *Editor-in-chief, Comments by Judges on Intellectual Property Cases, 6 volumes, Intellectual Property Press, 2003-2004.*
- *Co-author, Nutshell of Intellectual Property, People's Court Press, 2004.*
- *Editor-in-chief, Judicial Practice of Design Patent Invalidation and Infringement Cases, Law Press, 2005.*
- *Author, Chinese Patent Litigation, Intellectual Property Press, 2005.*
- *Author, Patent Disputes and Disposal, Intellectual Property Press, 2006.*
- *Editor-in-chief, Patent Law in Cases, Intellectual Property Press, 2008.*

Education
- *Bachelor in Economics, Economics Department, Beijing Normal University*
- *Master Program in Economic Law, Senior Judges Training Program, Peking University*
- *Graduate Program in Law, Adult Education College, Party School of the CPC Central Committee*

Judge Cheng was the deputy chief judge of the IP Tribunal of Beijing High People's Court before his retirement. Now he heads up a not-for-profit IP research institute in Beijing. Judge Cheng had published many books and articles related to China IP and his publications on China patent litigation were particularly very well received. Judge Cheng was once ranked one of the 50 most influential IP people by Managing Intellectual Property. On October 1st, 2010, we had a conversation with Judge Cheng in Beijing who has been publishing series of case collections in China to promote IP awareness. His organization has also done numerous IP research projects after his retirement from the bench.

Wen Xu: From your point of view, what do you think about the lots of misunderstandings of American mainstream IP field to Chinese IP by your years of experience in Sino-US IP exchange?

Cheng: *Misunderstandings do exist and are inevitable, but we also have problems. My attitude is that we must admit our own problems first then resolve misunderstandings. Once we gave a lecture to graduate students in US, a student asked: "There are lots of problems existing in China IP, aren't they? Are there many corrupted judges? Is infringement common?" A judge in our delegation to US denied firmly. He told the graduate students that no judges in China are corrupted and IP is protected adequately in China with compliments from all over the world. Then in my turn, I told the audience "The problems do exist in the protection of IP like corruption and infringement, but they are incidental." There is a Chinese old saying: Good news has no legs, but bad news has wings. That's why you got our negative news. If corruption and infringement are the mainstream, there will be no report and focus on it. I think it was our fault that we sometimes do not admit our own problems, which make others not believe us. The consequence is outrageous, and we need to reflect.*

Wen Xu: As an expert who works on the front line of IP, what is your view on the change of Chinese IP in the recent years?

Cheng: *There are a lot to say. Firstly, it is good that the public awareness of IP has been apparently improved since the National IP Strategy was implemented in 2008. IP is* *attached with great importance from enterprises to the entire nation. However, motivation mechanism has both negative and positives effects. Take patent as an example, the effect of patents has been placed emphasis since our country's implementation of science and technology strategy. But how many people understand the effect of patents on innovation? Just emphasizing the filing of patent applications had resulted in a great number of rubbish and low-standard patents, based on which can we conclude that we protect the invention and innovation? Patent holders can gain a huge amount of license fees under the American IPR system; companies like Coca Cola and McDonalds also receive significant amount in trademark licenses. How about China? The well known baby formula brand Sanlu disappeared with the collapse of the products. Whether such kind of IP has vitality invites our deep thinking.*

Wen Xu: There were several big patent litigation cases last year, e.g. *Chint vs Schneider* utility model case. Could you please tell us why there was outbreak of so many big cases in 2008?

Cheng: *I should not be commenting a pending case which now is going through appeal procedures.*

[**Editorial Note:** Chint and Schneider settled their suits in China and worldwide for about RMB157.5 million yuan in April 2009]

Zhejiang Court has adjudicated several important IP cases in 2008 in which all Chinese plaintiffs won and foreign defendants lost. The cases were all sensitive including the case you just mentioned. In first instance, Schneider was ordered to pay RMB330 million yuan to the plaintiff. In Holley case, Samsung was ordered to pay RMB50 million yuan. In addition, the dress brand G2000 and the "Blue Storm" of Pepsi-Coke were all in trouble and the compensation had reached millions even ten millions. These cases showed us. 1) Awareness of intellectual property rights of enterprises is indeed enhanced including mainland enterprises in developed coastal areas who have been forced to grow up these years by foreign IP litigation. From legislators, law enforcement to administrative agencies and business persons in charge, they all have had awareness of IP protection to protect their own rights and interests; 2)

Western developed countries have had a great impact on China's IP legislation and improvement. Prior to publishing certain IP legislation amendments or judicial interpretations, legislators often go to America, Japan and Europe to solicit advice, which on the one hand could show our humbleness in learning from other countries, on the other hand, and more importantly, helps us to receive more international ideas to further improve China's IP system. The IP awareness of Chinese enterprises will be strengthened once the domestic IP system is improved. 3) With the 20 years' IP development in China, we really have had our own IP talents who not only have practical experience but also have right approaches to IP. We also learned from our repeated defeats by foreigners, and now we are well positioned to win. All of the above have evidenced the notable progress of China IP.

Wen Xu:	Do you have any concerns in addition to strengthening IP awareness?

Cheng: *I surely have some concerns. First we do not have enough IP jurisprudence experts. We have excellent patent experts, trademark experts and copyright experts, but I think there is still no authoritative IP jurisprudence experts in China. Thus, the value system of IP is quite lost. There are different understandings in the true meaning and function of IP. Simply copying others' system causes value lost, and the gap between theory and practice is pretty huge. This fundamental problem will gradually appear in the future and I am really worried about it. Next, in my opinion we already have a good legal system, however, our law enforcement is not satisfactory. The standards and the level of law enforcement are different. Even there are some cases reversing "black and white" which was fatal to our country's IP protection. After all, we can only look further when we stand higher. The IP value system must be resolved first in order to guide the improvement of IP practice in China.*

Wen Xu:	We heard a comment that in the IP area, the IP judges in Shanghai, Beijing, Guangzhou and Shenzhen are generally better than their peer lawyers in the region. How do you look at this issue?

Cheng: *I have not heard this before, but in my opinion, it is impossible. This relates to the role of the judges and lawyers. Judges are passive, waiting for both parties to present the facts, rarely take the initiative to research or investigate. Due to judicial power and discretion, the judges can choose to accept or reject an opinion. On the contrary, the lawyers are different-they have to actively research the cases and fight for their clients' interests. From this angle, the lawyers are more familiar with the cases they take on than presiding judges on the same cases. They also work harder in studying and researching laws and legal theories. Over time, the quality of the lawyers will improve. As for judges, they have more opportunities to attend trainings and education seminars than lawyers, but the effect can not be ascertained right now. I met some foreign lawyers who would study in details of a pose, a facial expression or a blink by a witness. Our IP professionals should learn from such a spirit of doing things. As for the education background, the IP judges in general have a slightly higher education than non-IP judges. They also have more opportunities to exchange with foreign IP professionals than other judges. But compared to the lawyers, this is not an advantage as lawyers also communicate with their foreign counterparts a lot. We have about 1,000 IP judges nationwide who are very young. It worries me . Lack of life experience will affect their ability to adjudicate cases. In comparison, lawyers who are more experienced in life and practice certainly have bigger advantages.*

Wen Xu: Do you think the global financial crisis has any impact on IP development?

Cheng: *There must be some impact, but temporarily it is not very obvious, Especially in China, economic development appears to be smooth. However, the impact to patent is very obvious for foreign enterprises. Foreign companies used to apply for a considerable number of patents, but now they just apply for important patents after financial crisis. After all, patent management and operation have costs. On the other hand, although we feel that the number of patent applications of foreign enterprises has decreased, IP litigation is growing quickly. A person in charge of a foreign company once stated " the whole world was no longer profitable during the financial crisis. Since we have applied so many patents in China, it is the time to claim our rights." What he stated* *represents the business approach of some multinational enterprises at the moment.*

Wen Xu:	The new patent law has come into effect., As a patent expert, what is your opinion for this law and will it have significant impact on patent practice in China?

Cheng: *The foreign companies have studied the legislative changes of our patent law at a more in depth level than our domestic companies. They are more ready for the new law than domestic companies. For issues we discuss often, such as absolute novelty standard and national security review etc, foreign companies already have measures to deal with the changes. We are more worried about how the Chinese companies react under the new patent law. Our research shall focus on obtaining more good patents, better implementing the patents, and generating more profits and wealth with those patents for enterprises. In addition, after the implementation of the new patent law, the patent holders will pay more attention on how to really strengthen the protection of patents in China.*

Patent litigation takes dramatic step forward

IP litigation in China has been transformed, particularly because of the TRIPs Agreement. Now what the system need is foreign IP owners to start using it more, says judge Cheng Yongshun of the Beijing High Court, in an exclusive interview with Catherine Sun of Deacons, for MIP's China Guide.

As a new member of the WTO, China has recently amended its major IP laws, including its Patent Law, to comport with the requirements of the TRIPs Agreement. And the Supreme People's Court is in the process of making IP litigation more compatible with the provisions of the TRIPs Agreement. The progress of China's patent litigation system is very impressive, considering the fact that patent law in China is only about two decades old.

The recent interview with Honorable Judge Cheng Yongshun, the deputy chief judge of Beijing High Court No 3 (Intellectual Property) Tribunal, conducted by Catherine Sun of Deacon's Hong Kong office, on September 27 2002, highlighted the development of China's IP litigation system. The interview may provide a good outlook on the current patent litigation system, which makes it encouraging for foreign IP owners to litigate in China.

Ms. Sun:	How many patent actions are started each year?

Cheng: *From 1997 to the first half of 2002, about 7846 patent actions were started. After June 2001, the IP tribunals were merged into civil tribunals, so the IP cases adjudicated by the courts have no long had "ZHI" (IP) prefixes on their case numbers. Statistics for IP cases after 2001 have become more difficult to obtain and may be inaccurate, since IP cases are numbered as regular civil cases. For the past three years, about 5000 IP cases were filed each year, and patent cases were about one fifth of the total. For year 2002, the number of patent cases will exceed 1000 (one thousand).*

Ms. Sun:	How many patent actions accepted by courts went to trial?

Cheng: *In China, "trial" can embody different concepts. Courts in China can resolve a patent case in three different ways by going to "trial": first, by judgment, second, by settlement, and third, by withdrawal. A common law trial is similar to the first resolution by judgment, but in China, the other two resolutions also involve multiple hearings presided over by the courts. Only a few cases would be settled without courts' intervention.*

[Therefore, Judge Cheng believes that more than 90% of patent actions go to trial ultimately].

Cheng: *Two circumstances will delay the trial for one or more years: first, where a foreign entity is a party, and second, where the subject matter involves complex technology.*

Ms. Sun: Who may assert a patent?

• **Ms. Sun:** Patentee?

Cheng: *Yes*

• **Ms. Sun:** Assignee?

Cheng: *Yes*

• **Ms. Sun:** Exclusive licensee?

Cheng: *Yes*

• **Ms. Sun:** Non-exclusive licensee?

Cheng: *Yes, but only if patent holders grants non-exclusive licenses the right to sue.*

Ms. Sun: What is the cost of a patent action?

Cheng: *Court fees depend on the damages claimed, according to a formula specified in the law, somewhat like the US income tax rate.*

> *Attorneys' fee are negotiated by the parties based on the amount of damages, and normally are between 10% and 15%.*

Ms. Sun:	Who represents the parties – attorneys-at-law, patent agents, or both?

Cheng: *Attorneys-at-law; patent agents; foreign attorneys, who must be Chinese nationals, acting as citizen representatives, or Chinese citizens can represent the parties.*

Ms. Sun:	What is the average time from the filing of the action to the start of the trial?

Cheng: *For a first instance trial, according to the civil procedure rules, patent cases involving only domestic entities or persons, must be completed within six months. For an appeal, the completion time is three months. Two circumstances will delay the trial for one or more years: first, where a foreign entity is a party, and second, where the subject matter involves complex technology.*

Ms. Sun:	What is the average length of a trial?

Cheng: *On average a half day (four hours) trial is likely. Complex cases might take one to two days.*

Ms. Sun:	What is the average time from the close of the trial to the judgment?

Cheng: *Chinese courts try to hand down the judgments at the close of trial. But now it normally takes one to two months in patent cases. For complex patent cases, it might take two to three months.*

Cheng: *One of the other ideas behind the court was not that it would help curb IP infringement necessarily, but that IP litigation would be handled more efficiently and predictably*

Ms. Sun:	What is the percentage of patents found valid and infringed?

• Ms. Sun:	Overall?

Cheng: *About 60%.*

• **Ms. Sun:**   Where the patent owner is foreign?

Cheng: *Foreign patent holders file very few patent cases. In the last decade there have been no more 30 altogether. The infringement percentage should be higher than 60%.*

• **Ms. Sun:**   Where the defendant is foreign?

Cheng: *Only a few cases have been filed. Infringement should be around 60%.*

Ms. Sun: What is the percentage of patents found invalid (revoked) at trial?

• **Ms. Sun:**   Overall?

Cheng: *From 1988 to June 2001, there were 135 cases invalidating inventions were received, and about 20% of the cases were reversed, modified or remanded.*

• **Ms. Sun:**   Where the patent owner is foreign?

Cheng: *No obvious difference, about 20%*

• **Ms. Sun:**   Where the defendant is foreign?

Cheng: *About 20%*

Ms. Sun: What is the percentage of patent judgments appealed to the Court of Appeals?

Cheng: *In China, settlements and withdrawals, adjudicated by trial courts, are consented to by the parties, thus parties normally do not appeal. Only judgments are appealed. About 30% of judgments are appealed.*

Ms. Sun: What is the percentage of patent cases reversed in the Court of Appeals on validity?

Cheng: *About 20%-30%.*

Ms. Sun: What is the percentage of patent cases reversed in the Court of Appeals on infringement?

Cheng: *About 20%-30%.*

Ms. Sun: What is the cost of appeal of a patent decision?

Cheng: *Same as a trial.*
Court fees depend on the damages claimed according to a formula specified by law, somewhat like U.S. income tax rate. Attorney's fees are negotiated by the parties based on amount of damages, and normally are 10%-15%.

Ms. Sun: How many petitions are made to the Supreme People's Court regarding patent cases each year?

Cheng: *Very few IP cases are petitioned to the Supreme People's High Court each year, so patent cases are even fewer.*

Ms. Sun: How many patent cases are heard by the Supreme People's Court in China?

Cheng: *None as a first instance court.*

Ms. Sun: What precedential value (if any) does the court attach to judgments in other jurisdictions?

Cheng: *None. Judges are not bound by decisions or judgments rendered by sister courts, higher courts, or even the Supreme People's Court. Previous decisions or judgments are for reference only.*

Ms. Sun: How are the damages decided in China?

Cheng: *Damages are generally based on actual damages suffered by patent holders or actual profits made by infringers, plus reasonable investigation cost. Attorneys' fees are rarely awarded. If none of the above can be quantified, the courts normally award a statutory damage of not more than $60,000.*

Ms. Sun:	Are opinions sought as a defence to infringement or willful infringement?

Cheng:	*No. Since there are no enhanced damages (such as treble damages plus attorneys' fees) provisions for willful infringement, accused or potential infringers do not normally seek non-infringement or invalidity opinions.*

Ms. Sun:	Is IP litigation insurance available in China?

Cheng:	*No. I've never heard of it in China.*

Ms. Sun:	What procedures are there for depositions and discovery?

Cheng:	*Exchange of evidence is available in China, but is not as extensive, formal and sophisticated as in the U.S. There are no deposition, production of documents and interrogatories procedures in China.*

Ms. Sun:	Are experts used and who appoints them?

Cheng:	*Both parties and courts can appoint experts. Experts appointed by parties must be consented to by both parties. Courts do not have to consult parties when consulting or retaining experts.*

Ms. Sun:	Are validity and infringement heard at trial together or separately?

Cheng:	*Validity and infringement are bifurcated.*

Ms. Sun:	Are damages decided at trial at the same time as liability?

Cheng:	*If parties do not request bifurcation, damages and liability are decided at the same time.*

Ms. Sun:	What forms of alternative dispute resolution are used?

Cheng: *Alternative dispute resolution mechanisms such as reconciliation, mediation, arbitration and administrative adjudication are used frequently in China.*

Judge Xu Jianchu

Time and Place:	August 23, 2007 11:30am-2:00pm @ Shanghai in a restaurant near Judge Xu's home
Attendees:	Catherine Sun, Managing Partner, Foley & Lardner LLP Shanghai Office Victor Xue, IP author and scholar Harold Wegner, Professor, George Washington University Law School Wen Xu, currently a law student of Northwestern University Law School Xiao Xu, Judge Xu's daughter, currently an undergraduate student of China Eastern University of Law and Politics

Late Judge Xu was the chief judge of Shanghai High People's Court No. 3 (IP) Tribunal who had played instrumental role in shaping the IP judicial protection system in Shanghai. Judge Xu passed away on March 21st, 2009 and our interview which was conducted after he came back to work from his surgery was the last piece of his insight and statement on IP. We dedicate this piece to Judge Xu and his family. Further, there is a Judge Xu Jianchu Intellectual Property Scholarship being set up at the China Eastern University of Politics and Law in 2009 to sponsor 10 IP students each year who will be interested in joining IP judiciary after graduation.[1]

Below interview was originally conducted in Chinese and the English translation was unedited from the original interview.

Ms. Sun:	Will a Chinese court discriminate against a foreign company in an IP case?

Judge Xu: *First, my colleagues and myself do not differentiate litigation parties based on their country origin. The court system is*

---

[1] The donation information for Judge Xu Jianchu IP Scholarship is as follow:
Name of the Account: China Eastern University of Politics and Law
Account Number: 1001223609026407097
Bank: 022236 Yuyuan Road Brunch, Shanghai of Industry and Commerce Bank of China (ICBC)

pushing the members of the judiciary to adjudicate cases to the best of their ability. However, some local courts may be influenced by other aspects such as local interests.

Second, the promotion of IP protection is an important aspect of national IP strategy. The national interest plays a very key role in ruling IP cases. Judges will consider international impact when making decisions for IP cases especially for foreign-based cases and related cases.

Third, because of the sensitive nature, the foreign related IP cases are always adjudicated by top judges who always have more advanced legal skills and better understanding of IP laws and regulations.

Wegner: *The foreign party will never blame itself for a loss, but instead will often say that the local courts are to blame. Sometimes, the foreign parties do not prepare adequately to manage cases in foreign courts; but after they have lost a case, they will only say they have faced discrimination by local courts. The foreign parties often do not understand the local legal procedures, local cultural differences. Whose fault is this for losing the case? The classic example is the Japanese Manmade Diamond case where the American attorney slept during the court hearing.*

Ms. Sun: What can be the measures of punishment for IP infringers in China?

Judge Xu: *First, criminal punishment: In China, a patent infringer can be jailed for up to 7 years.*

Second, misdemeanor punishment: some IP infringers will be charged for violation of public security regulations if they did not meet the criminal thresholds.

Third, civil punishment: the principal for civil damages in China is "compensatory" not "punitive"; this is not a way to punish an infringer but to instead compensate the property rights owner. In the United States, only intentional patent infringement can be basis for a judgment of punitive damages. In China, only the Law of the People's Republic of China on Protection of Consumer Rights and Interests sets the punitive damages principal for an act of intentional cheating to effectively protect the consumer rights and interests ("Double compensation"). However, the definition of what is a consumer is limited to a very narrow scope so domestic merchants will not be regarded as a consumer in China.

Wegner: *In the United States, there is also a debate between public interest and local consumer interest, for example, the eBay case in the United States Supreme Court. The extent to which an injunction should be granted is now under discussion for IP cases in the wake of eBay.*

Ms. Sun: It is hard to obtain evidence for IP infringement cases. What is the court's attitude towards such a reality?

Judge Xu: *In China, the ways to investigate patent infringement are quite limited. Chinese lawyers are not trained as professionals for the difficult task of collecting evidence. This can be regarded as a "Unstable Time" for free competition. Moreover, there is no discovery procedure available as part of a court proceeding. The new patent law is planning to increase the maximum statutory damages to one million RMB versus half million RMB under the existing patent law now. An investigation company may help the property rights owner and the lawyers collect evidence, although it is not legitimate to run an investigation business in China. The court will accept the evidence collected by investigation companies – or we say consulting company – if the evidence was achieved legally.*

Ms. Sun: You mentioned investigation company. Is it acceptable to use the evidence gained by investigation companies?

Judge Xu: *We will accept such evidence which can show an evidentiary chain and can strongly prove the facts. You can refer to the basic evidence rules that we have learned in law school. There is a case where the defendant argued that the notarized trapped purchase designed on purpose by the property rights owner with a notarization official who was not wearing his uniform during the process. We discussed the case and finally determined that this can be accepted as the notarization evidence because the notarization official can be casually dressed for the purpose of doing some secret evidence notarization. If the defendant contended it was a customized purchase trap by the property rights owner, then the burden of proof would be switched to the defendant.*

Now the voice recording or video tape can be accepted by a court as evidence unless it is collected in bad faith in a manner that infringed the rights of others. If it is too difficult for the property rights owners to collect evidence, they can apply for evidence preservation before or during the lawsuit. Evidence preservation is widely used in China; the Judges are skilled in handling such matters, such as how to choose the best time to execute evidence preservation and how to recover damaged computer data.

The Trademark Office released a new version of NICE trademark classification and the news media widely misreported that "China has allowed setting up investigation companies, because the new version of trademark classification has a classification for "investigation service". Actually, you can apply for an investigation company but the Agency for Industry and Commerce (AIC) will not issue you the business license to do it.

Ms. Sun: *Our practice to clean the evidence collected by an investigation company is to use the sighting report to file a complaint to a local AIC for a raid and after that AIC will issue a punishment decision. The punishment decision can be accepted by the court for convincing the judges for the infringement.*

Ms. Sun: What kind of evidence submitted is sufficient to warrant the evidence preservation?

Judge Xu: *If you have prima facie evidence then you can apply for evidence preservation. The prima facie evidence means the basic infringement facts and the specific target. The approval rate is actually quite high. However, if you file a complaint to the Copyright Bureau, they will collect evidence for you; but they will be reluctant to make punishment decisions. Because if they punish someone wrongfully, they will face an administrative lawsuit; which is really quite serious for them. Sometimes, you can ask them to help. For AIC, they always issue punishment decisions by themselves because they are powerful enough to stop others from suing them for wrongful punishment.*

In 2003 interview conducted by Ms. Sun with Judge Xu on behalf of Managing Intellectual Property, Judge Xu stated on this issue: We understand that the requesting party does not have the evidence to be preserved when making such a request, so evidence submitted should reasonably persuade the court that the other side has such evidence and it is likely to be destroyed. But the evidence submitted must be legally obtained. We once dismissed an evidence preservation request based on an illegal acquisition of the evidence. The requesting party hired Hong Kong investigator to conduct a thorough investigation of the opposing party in Shanghai, and submitted the investigation report to court. Because Hong Kong investigators cannot conduct business in Shanghai, we dismissed the request. Had the investigation been done by a PRC company, we would have approved the evidence preservation request.

Ms. Sun: Is there a conflict between the *prima facie* evidence and evidence preservation? We can not bring a lawsuit without sufficient evidence.

Judge Xu: *You can also choose to apply for evidence preservation during the lawsuit and the judge will send the complaint and the evidence preservation document to the defendant at the same time to ensure that the evidence will not be destroyed after service.*

Ms. Sun: When we deal with such evidence obtained through investigation companies, we may have to "clean up such evidence" in order for them to be admissible. What is your advice for such a "clean up procedure"?

Judge Xu: *We will decide the validity of the evidence on a case by case basis. There is a case involving Microsoft that happened just days ago. Microsoft assigned a Hong Kong based investigation company to carry out evidence collection for their company but during the court hearing, I asked them to provide the investigators' personal signatures to prove the evidence was collected legally because the defendant raised the concern of an "investigation trap". However, being afraid of other punishment made from governmental agencies for illegal business crime, the investigators did not want to even sign their names on the report as evidence.*

Wegner: *The scope of the discovery is widely discussed not only in United States but also in England where Lord Justice Jacob suggested that British law should involve a narrower scope of the discovery for the purpose of saving money and time during a trial.*

Judge Xu: *The PRC Civil Procedure Law will be amended soon but the focus of the revision is on enforcement of judgment not on evidence and procedure for evidence. I don't think the new version of the Civil Procedure Law will add a United States style discovery procedure; and, moreover, China is a code law country and we will not follow former cases of others. However, there are some infant discovery rules in China Civil Procedure Law: If one party can prove that the other party has certain documents but refused to show to the court, the court may draw an unfavorable inference toward that party.*

Actually, in the evidence regulations, we have set the rules for collecting evidence, evidence discovery and evidence exchange. In my court, both parties can exchange evidence in front of the court. Such rules are just starting to be applied in practice but are still not widely used on a national basis.

Ms. Sun: *Judge Xu conducted some discovery experiments in the past. He gave the parties 30 days to exchange the evidence, and then made trial exhibit lists on all evidence exchanged. During the hearing, each party can dispute the other's exhibits. Judge Xu had the discretion not to admit the disputed evidence.*

Wegner: Can a United States judgment be regarded as evidence in China court? Can we do a "deposition" in China?

Judge Xu: *There are two major parts of a Chinese judgment and one is the fact part and other is the reasoning part. As far as I know, the US judgments include all the detailed facts and will be of great help in a Chinese court after it is legalized and notarized.*

The deposition can be taken at an embassy. If there is a bilateral agreement or an international convention where both countries are members, then they can do the "deposition" in China through specific procedure. There are quite a few bilateral agreements between China and other countries but most of them relate to serving of court documents, and not to investigation. For the settlement made in the United States, we will consider the matter on a case by case basis, as there are no specific rules for using a settlement result here.

Wegner:	Is the "Doctrine of Equivalent" (DOE) widely used in patent lawsuits in China?

Judge Xu: *Actually, in practice, the DOE is not widely adopted in Chinese courts. There is still a debate among IP scholars about what should be deemed to be patent infringement, so the court will use the DOE in a very cautious manner. Chinese Judges regard the DOE as one of the methods to determine infringement or to confirm non-infringement. The Supreme People's Court does not show a positive attitude to the DOE. But, at least, it has not ruled against the DOE so that judges can choose to apply the DOE when adjudicating a patent infringement case.*

Wegner: *The DOE in the United States was extremely powerful at one time but now has been greatly weakened. During 1980s and 1990s, DOE had a stronger influence in patent cases but more and more Judges are not applying the DOE in their judgment of patent cases.*

Wegner:	How does one prove "process patent" infringement? For example in Japan effluent waste water samples are sometimes analyzed.

Judge Xu: *The method of calculating derivative products can help to prove the infringement and for the new product patent process, the burden of proof is reversed to defendant.*

Taken the Viagra case as an example, China actually is not the first country to invalidate the Viagra patent; a UK court has done so. The press widely reported the Viagra case as a "political" case in China because the foreign patent right was defeated by the Chinese court. We felt that it was unfair for China to be scrutinized like this. In the Viagra case, the patent document did not provide the public with sufficient information about the drug, so it was reasonable for the judge to agree to invalidate the patent.

[Ms. Sun also raised several questions of the case GM vs. Cherry.]

Judge Xu explained that in China one can apply for a design patent for a car model but not a real car itself. The car design can only be protected by the Anti-Unfair Competition Law but the newly issued judicial interpretation provided "reverse engineering" defense for a trade secret infringement case.

Judge Xu: *I handled a case which was filed by a Canadian movie media editor machine company that claimed that a Chinese company infringed its machine patent and sold the machines in China. Finally the court ruled that the infringer pay the highest statutory 500,000 RMB as damages; but, the Canadian company still was not satisfied with the result because the infringing machine was valued in the millions in the Canadian market: But, the Canadian company never did sell its machine in China. The Canadian market price cannot be used for calculating damages in China so we cannot support their claims for a huge amount of damages.*

Ms. Sun: Can a party file so called declaratory judgment?

Judge Xu: *In China, we also can file a lawsuit for a declaration of non-infringement. But such a lawsuit can only be filed after someone receives a cease and desist letter or there are other existing IP claims. The Peter Rabbit case in China is an example.*

Ms. Sun: How many lawsuits are handled in Shanghai per year? What is the percentage with respect to the entire country?

Judge Xu: *Guangdong has the most IP cases, particularly for design patents. Most of the IP cases in Shanghai are for trademark and copyright infringement. Frankly speaking, Shanghai does not have many IP cases, about 800-900 cases per year.*

Ms. Sun: What is the percentage of judges with legal background in your court?

Judge Xu: *After the Judge Law became effective, all the judges should pass the judicial qualification examination but those who were appointed as judges before the Judge Law will still act as*

66

judges. Nowadays, the high court seldom recruits fresh graduates except for some doctor degree graduates but rather directly selects good judges from the local courts or intermediate courts.

Ms. Sun: What subject matter jurisdiction does your own court have?

Judge Xu: *We normally take appeals from the intermediate courts. But for cases with disputed amounts over RMB 100 million, or with a significant impact in Shanghai, we have discretion to take the case as a court of first instance.*

Ms. Sun: Will China open the door for foreign law firms to practice in China in the near future?

Judge Xu: *I don't think so. Foreign law firm practice will be limited to certain areas for a long period. If a foreign lawyer is also an employee of a party which is a foreign company, that lawyer can appear not as a lawyer, but as an employee representing that company.*

If a foreign lawyer is a Chinese citizen, he or she may appear not as a lawyer, but as a citizen. This is so called "citizen representation" under the rules of civil procedure. The most important issue is that a citizen representation cannot involve any attorney's fees, except for certain expenses.

Ms. Sun: Will judgments issued by other courts influence your decision?

Judge Xu: *As we all know China is a code law system country so the earlier cases do not have formal case law effect. As there exist different levels of courts, the superior courts' decision or opinion will count a lot to lower level courts. The Supreme Court began to send good judgments to the lower courts for guidance and reference; in fact, the lower courts do follow these opinions in adjudicating cases within their jurisdiction.*

Rules of Engagement for IP Litigation

The late Hon. Jianchu Xu, was former chief judge of the Shanghai Higher People's Court IP (No. 3) Tribunal. Judge Xu had been a talented IP judge in China in helping to shape Shanghai's IP enforcement landscape.

In 1996, Judge Xu spent six months in the chambers of the Hon. Randall R. Rader of the Court of Appeals for the Federal Circuit, where he began a long friendship with George Washington University Law School graduate student and then lawyer, Catherine Sun. Ms. Sun was involved with various cooperative efforts with Judge Xu for improvement of global patent relations. She introduced the work of Judge Xu to the international patent community in an interview published in 2003 in Managing Intellectual Property.

The **Rules of Engagement for IP Litigation** article appeared in Managing Intellectual Property Magazine May 2003. The interview is copyright Deacons Hong Kong and is reprinted with kind permission of Deacons.

More and more companies are launching IP litigation in China. Before they do so, they should be aware of what is and what isn't allowed in a Chinese courtroom as Judge Xu, a prominent IP Judge in Shanghai, explains in an interview.

Catherine Sun of Deacons' Hong Kong office first met Honourable Judge Xu Jianchu, the chief judge of Shanghai High People's Court No 3 Civil Tribunal (Intellectual Property Tribunal) in 1996 at the US Court of Appeals for the Federal Circuit in Washington, DC, where she was a judicial intern, while Judge Xu was a visiting judge observing US IP litigation practice at the same court. They met again in Shanghai in March 2003 for this exclusive interview for MIP.

Ms. Sun:	How many No 3 Civil Tribunals (IP Tribunals) are there in Shanghai?

Judge Xu: *There are five IP tribunals in Shanghai. We have two intermediate people's courts, and each of them has a No 3 Civil Tribunal. My tribunal is in Shanghai People's Court,* *and it is an appellate IP court. The other two IP tribunals are in district people's courts: one in Pudong new area, and the other in Huangpu district.*

Ms. Sun: I remember that only intermediate people's courts have jurisdiction over patent cases. Why does Shanghai also have two IP courts at district people's court level?

Judge Xu: *The Supreme People's Court, the highest court of the country, once issued a notice, stating that patent cases at the first instance should be adjudicated by intermediate courts in the capital city of each province, and the four autonomous metropolitan cities (Beijing, Shanghai, Tianjin and Chongqing). The Supreme People's Court also designated a few non-capital cities' intermediate courts to have jurisdiction over patent cases, such as Qingdao, Dalian, Yantai, Wenzhou and Fushun, and non-capital cities in special economic zones, such as Shenzhen, Zhuhai, Shantou and Xiamen. These courts also have exclusive jurisdiction over plant variety rights and layout designs of integrated circuits.*
Several district courts such as Beijing Haidan, Chaoyang, and Shanghai Pudong and Huangpu, are also designated as IP courts. But these courts only have jurisdiction over trade mark, copyright and unfair competition cases. No patent cases, or plant variety and layout design cases, can be accepted by these courts.

Ms. Sun: How many IP cases are accepted in Shanghai annually?

Judge Xu: *It used to be 600-700 a year. This year it might exceed 800.*

Ms. Sun: Do you see an increase in IP cases involving foreign companies post WTO?

Judge Xu: *Yes, but mainly involving trade mark, domain name, computer software and design patents in Shanghai. I spoke in 1996 at a Seattle conference and told the audience at the time that there was no single IP case filed by a US company in Shanghai, and only one IP case filed against a US company pre-1996. Now, there are many foreign companies litigating in Shanghai, such as Microsoft, Adobe and Unilever.*

Ms. Sun:	What differences do you see between the IP courts in Beijing and the IP courts in Shanghai?

Judge Xu: *There are not many patent cases involving inventions filed in Shanghai. Beijing gathers more talent in IP: research institutes, universities, foreign companies, and returnees. Beijing intermediate people's courts have exclusive jurisdiction over the validity and patentability appeals on the decisions made by the Patent Office, so the IP courts in Beijing have more experience and exposure in patent cases involving complex technology. Beijing intermediate people's courts also have exclusive jurisdiction over trade mark and copyright appeals from the relevant administrative offices.*

Ms. Sun:	How is a judgment finally made in an IP court?

Judge Xu: *Normally one judge, or even a number of judges are assigned to a case. They make decisions in IP cases. There is an adjudication committee in each court, formed by the chief judge of the IP tribunal, and other senior ranked judges of that court. For an exceptional case where a unanimous decision is impossible or if the decision has significant impact in Shanghai, the adjudication committee would review a panel's decision and make the final decision.*

Ms. Sun:	What subject matter jurisdiction do Shanghai IP courts have?

Judge Xu: *Shanghai IP courts do not have jurisdiction over appeals on decisions made by the Chinese Intellectual Property Office, Trademark Office, and Copyright Office in Beijing. Other than that, we take almost all other kinds of IP disputes.*

Ms. Sun:	What subject matter jurisdiction does your own court have?

Judge Xu: *We normally take appeals from the intermediate courts. But for cases with disputed amounts over Rmb100 million (about $12 million), or with significant impact in Shanghai, we have discretion to take the case at first instance.*

Ms. Sun:	How can a plaintiff satisfy personal jurisdiction and venue requirements?

Judge Xu: *In order for Shanghai IP courts to accept a case, a defendant must reside or have places of business in Shanghai, the contract must be performed in Shanghai, or infringing activities must be conducted in Shanghai.*

Ms. Sun: Could a case be dismissed for lack of jurisdiction or improper venue?

Judge Xu: *Before an answer is filed, a defendant can challenge jurisdiction and / or venue. If the challenge is successful, we would transfer the case to a proper sister court. We do not dismiss a case outright for these reasons.*

Ms. Sun: You have observed US-style discovery. Do you think China will eventually have that kind of discovery in place?

Judge Xu: *I don't think so. It is too expensive for China.*

Ms. Sun: What about adopting a quasi-discovery practice to provide at least some opportunities to the parties and litigants to discover the facts of the case?

Judge Xu: *It is possible. I actually have conducted some discovery experiments in the past. I have given the parties 30 days to exchange the evidence, and then we made trial exhibits lists on all evidence exchanged. During the hearing, each party can dispute the other party's exhibits. I have the discretion not to admit the excluded evidence.*

Ms. Sun: When do you conduct such evidence exchange?

Judge Xu: *It is done before the trial, sortly after an answer is filed. If one party would like more time, a 30-day extension could be granted.*

Ms. Sun: But I can imagine that parties would only produce documents that would support their claims, not

> documents against their own position. How you deal with that?

Judge Xu: *That's right. Parties only submit documents in favor of their positions. One party cannot compel the other party to produce documents. But if only one party requests the other party to produce certain documents, and the other party says they do not have them, the documents are deemed to be nonexistent. The refusing party cannot later use these documents to advance their position.*

Ms. Sun: How do you prevent destruction of evidence?

Judge Xu: *If one party can prove the other party has destroyed certain documents, then the court may draw an unfavorable inference toward that party. The court can also refer an evidence destruction case to prosecutors for criminal action, but it has no power to sanction the lawyers or party directly.*

Ms. Sun: Would it help if China imposes and enforces stricter rules of professional conduct regulating lawyers?

Judge Xu: *Definitely. We judges have a code of professional conduct. Several years ago, a judge in Shanghai was arrested for receiving bribes, but the several lawyers who offered bribes walked away. There are two different systems regulating the conduct of lawyers and judges. Judges have no right to sanction lawyers directly in China.*

Ms. Sun: Is the concept of attorney-client privilege or attorney work product recognized in China?

Judge Xu: *Since China does not have formal discovery, these principles are not particularly useful in litigation. Courts can not compel the parties to produce evidence, let alone the attorneys.*

Ms. Sun: Are interrogatories, request for admission and depositions available in China?

Judge Xu: *No.*

Ms. Sun: Is it possible to adopt certain mechanisms to offer parties other discovery tools? For instance, to provide each party limited numbers of interrogatories and requests for admissions, or to provide court-supervised depositions to key witnesses?

Judge Xu: *Yes, but there is nothing addressing these mechanisms in Chinese procedural and evidential rules. So maybe the Supreme People's Court should issue some sort of judicial interpretation in order to have nationwide effect. It could be done through the stipulation of parties, but judges would need to know exactly how to do it.*

Ms. Sun: Do you think common law discovery training programmes for judges would be helpful?

Judge Xu: *Yes that would be useful. There is a judge training centre in Shanghai which orgainizes training programmes and deals with interested foreign parties. A lot of my younger colleagues have a better grasp of English, so they are very eager to learn new things.*

Ms. Sun: What do judges do on a daily basis?

Judge Xu: *Fifty per cent of my time is spent on cases, and fifty per cent on meetings, travel, talks and other administrative matters.*

Ms. Sun: Do you think it is possible to select judges from experienced lawyers in China?

Judge Xu: *Right now there are several unresolved issues. first, many judges who do not have a law degree or previous legal training are already in the system. It may take some time to phase these people out. Second, right now all judges, prosecutors and lawyers must past national unified judicial exams in order to become a judge, a prosecutor or a lawyer.*

But these three professions are not freely transferrable. When the system allows judges and public prosecutors to switch career more easily, it may be possible. Third, lawyers are a lot better paid than judges and prosecutors so there is no incentive for lawyers to become judges.

Ms. Sun:	Do you allow foreign lawyers to appear before your court?

Judge Xu: *If a foreign lawyer appears alone as a lawyer, we would try to persuade the party to retain a Chinese lawyer. A foreign lawyer definitely can come to a hearing, if it is a public hearing.*

If a foreign lawyer is also an employee of a party which is a foreign company or a foreign investment enterprise in China, that lawyer can appear not as a lawyer, but as an employee representing that company.

If a foreign lawyer is a Chinese citizen, he or she may appear not as a lawyer, but as a citizen. This is so-called "citizen representation" under the rules of civil procedure.

Ms. Sun:	Do you allow *ex parte* communication by counsel?

Judge Xu: *No. We have a judge's code of conduct, prohibiting ex parte communication. Otherwise judges are subject to disciplinary sanctions.*

Ms. Sun:	What are the remedies for the adversely affected party where the opposing party made an *ex parte* communication with the court?

Judge Xu: *The adversely affected party may request to replace the judge who was contacted by the other party.*

Ms. Sun:	Do you give substantial weight to opinions rendered by a court-appointed authenticator or expert?

Judge Xu: *The authenticator's opinion or expert's opinion or expert's opinion is part of the indirect evidence. I would have to review and weigh all the evidence presented before I could make a decision.*

Ms. Sun: What are the differences between an authenticator and an expert?

Judge Xu: *An authenticator is a court-certified witness who authenticates the evidence. There is a list of judicially recognised authenticating authorities. Authenticators are associated with these authorities and retained by the court or parties to issue authenticating opinions.*

Experts are not court certified. Either or both the court and the parties can retain experts. Experts normally provide testimony or written reports on complex technology issues. There is no judicially recognized list of experts. The losing party has to pay the fees of a court-appointed authenticator or expert.

Ms. Sun: Can parties challenge the authenticator's opinion or expert's opinion?

Judge Xu: *Yes. The parties can challenge their qualifications and conclusions.*

Ms. Sun: Is a damages expert used in China IP litigation?

Judge Xu: *This is not popular. The court may sometimes seize a party's financial records for auditing, upon written request of the other party. The auditing entity normally is the court-appointed expert.*

Ms. Sun: Sometimes the parties apply to the court to preserve certain evidence of the opposing side. What kind of evidence submitted is sufficient to warrant such evidence preservation?

Judge Xu: *We understand that the requesting party does not have the evidence to be preserved when making such a request, so evidence submitted should reasonably persuade the court that the other side has such evidence and it is likely to be destroyed. But the evidence submitted must be legally obtained. We once dismissed an evidence preservation request based on an illegal acquisition of the evidence. The requesting party hired a Hong Kong investigator to conduct a thorough investigation of the opposing party in Shanghai, and submitted the investigation report to the court. Because Hong Kong investigators cannot conduct business in Shanghai, we dismissed the request. Had the investigation been done by a PRC company, we would have to preserve the evidence preservation request.*

Ms. Sun: Are statutory damages granted frequently?

Judge Xu: *Yes.*

Ms. Sun: Do you think a high damages award is possible in China?

Judge Xu: *Yes, damages are subject to proof. Since there are not many high-value patents litigating in China, no cases have provided an adequate basis for rendering a high damages award.*

Zhang Guangliang

Time and Place:	Beijing Summer 2007
Attendees:	Victor Xue, IP author and scholar Wen Xu, currently a law student of Northwestern University Law School

Mr. Zhang Guangliang, PhD, Peking University; LLM, John Marshall Law School; LLB, People's University of China ; B.A, Anhui University, had been working in Beijing First Intermediate People's Court as clerk, judge, acting chief judge of the Intellectual Property Tribunal, director of the Research Department and Member of the Court Judicial Committee from July 1994 to June 2007. Dr. Zhang teaches at China University of Political Science & Law, and concurrently serves as the Managing Associate Director of the Institute for International Intellectual Property of Peking University, guest research fellow of the IPR Development & Research Center of the State Intellectual Property Office, and adjunct professor of the John Marshall Law School (USA) since July 2007. His publications include English-Chinese & Chinese-English Intellectual Property Protection Dictionary, Issues & Cases in Intellectual Property Enforcement, Civil Remedies for Intellectual Property Infringement, and the Study on the Application & Protection of Intellectual Property.

Mr. Zhang now is an associate profession of China University of Political Science and Law and was a former judge from Beijing No.1 Intermediate People's Court. Mr. Zhang graduated from Renmin University of China in 1994 and double majored in intellectual property law and English. In 1999, Mr. Zhang graduated from the John Marshall Law School with a master degree.

Victor Xue:	From my understanding, you were a Judge in Beijing No. 1 Intermediate People's Court. Why did you choose to become a scholar after your long term service at bench?

| Zhang: | *I am really interested in researching and studying intellectual property issues, which was my major research field from my undergraduate to doctoral study, which is not common in* |

China. I worked very well in the court which experience improved me to a judge with comprehensive knowledge and experience. However, I really like to focus on IP issues and IP related cases instead of handling all sorts of cases, such as criminal cases and other kinds of civil cases. This is the major reason why I chose to switch my career from a judge to a professor. I want to spend more time on researching IP issues, and I believe only a law school could provide me such an environment.

Victor Xue:	As an expert in the IP field, could you please share with us your previous experiences in this field as a judge?

Zhang: *From my perspective, many foreigners do have certain misunderstandings with China IP judicial practice. During the first 5 years after joining WTO, China adopted TRIPS to determine intellectual property cases. Each officer in the governmental or judicial departments attached lots of importance to intellectual property issues. Majority of IP laws were amended according to the WTO requirements. We strictly comply with and enforce the relevant IP laws and regulations. Sometimes, our enforcement is way too strict. For example, it is really hard to request a preliminary injunction order in US and the successful rate is only around 3%. But the successful rate for requesting a preliminary injunction is approximately 80% to 90% in China. Further, even though the plaintiff is unlikely to win in China, it is still possible to obtain a preliminary injunction order from the court. In the United States, only if the judge can ensure the plaintiff's victory of the case, the judge could grant a preliminary injunction order. According to Mr. Zhang's article: from 2002 to 2006, Beijing No 1 Intermediate People's Court accepted 2,427 cases inclusive of the first instance and appeal civil cases, and 283 of the cases were foreign related cases. Among the first instance civil cases, parties in 40% of the cases filed requests for various of temporary relief measures. For the requests which were in compliance with the law and regulations, Beijing No.1 intermediate People's Court promptly took appropriate measures to ensure the enforcement of the right owners' procedural rights.*

From the criminal punishment perspective, China did well too. In 2006, 3,587 individuals were sentenced for criminal liability due to IP infringement. There is a chapter specializing on IP crime in the current criminal law.

Compared with the US judicial process, the Chinese judicial process is more efficient. In practice, a foreign related IP case does not exceed nine months which includes the civil litigation process and other notarization and legalization process.

Victor Xue: Have you ever adjudicated any foreign related patent cases?

Zhang: *Sure, I actually have done a lot of such cases. I was the chief judge in Chery case and Pfizer case which had a big influence on China IP field. According to Mr. Zhang's article. from 2002 to 2006, Beijing No 1 Intermediate People's Court accepted 2,016 IP administrative cases in total, among which there were 1,447 patent administrative cases, and 659 trademark administrative cases. There were 671 foreign related trademark and patent cases, which accounted for 31.8% of total accepted cases. 2,064 IP administrative cases were decided, among which there were 1,440 patent administrative cases and 624 trademark administrative cases. 653 foreign related patent and trademark cases were decided, accounting for 31.6% of the total decided cases. The above number indicated that foreign related IP administrative cases accounted for a majority of the cases accepted. In fact, among the foreign related cases decided by the Beijing No. 1 Intermediate People's Court, the foreign parties won approximately 70% of the administrative cases and approximately 60% of the civil cases.*

Victor Xue: As to discovery procedure, could you introduce the practice in China?

Zhang: *As a matter of fact, China has certain discovery procedures which are similar to those in the US practice. For example, we have evidence preservation rules that the court can order the accused infringers to provide account books, audit reports and so on. Related rules have been clearly specified in the China Civil Evidence Rules. As for the timing of producing evidence , both parties can negotiate and usually the judge would respect the result reached by both parties. Meanwhile, both parties can negotiate the date of evidence exchange. Such rules have been quite maturely used in practice.*

| Victor Xue: | Foreign IP professionals always complain that damages awarded in an IP infringement case in China is extremely low. How do you think of it? |

Zhang: *About the damages, I admit that the absolute amount is low, but it relates to China's economic situation. If the court decides a relatively high damages award, the infringing party can not afford it and therefore it is unenforceable. Meanwhile, damages amount relates to the calculation method. If the plaintiff can not provide convincing evidence to support their claimed damages which are calculated based on the defendants' profits or the plaintiff's losses, the court has to calculate the damages amount according to the market value or license fee, or based on statutory damages. In absence of those data, the court can not order a relatively high damages in excess of certain limited amount.*

China IP system does not have punitive damages rules. Instead, our basic principle is to "compensatory" damages" Actually, punitive damage is not worldwide accepted in the IP field, For patent cases, only wilful infringement can trigger punitive damages. In China, normally half of one party's reasonable expense is born by the losing party. In US, each party is responsible for its own expense, and only under certain exceptional circumstances, the losing party is responsible for the other party's expense. Sometimes, the amount of reasonable expense is relatively high, and it is not calculated into the damages. In practice, the courts have decided certain high damages cases, such as the Yamaha case and Great Wall red wine case. For a pending patent case, the claimed damages are more than thirty million Yuan. According to Mr. Zhang's article, in the case that GMAC and ETC suing New Oriental School for copyright and trademark infringement of "GMAT", "GRE", "TOFEL", the court finally decided a 6.53 million Yuan in damages inclusive of the plaintiff's economic losses and reasonable expenses. This judgment sufficiently reflected the compensatory damages principle to the IP owners adopted by China IP courts.

| Victor Xue: | Can you talk about IP tribunal and IP judges? |

Zhang: *In this regard, frankly speaking, IP judges represent high-level judges in the court system. Only high-quality judges* can be involved in IP cases. Additionally, the courts attach importance to the training of IP judges, and often offer both domestic trainings and overseas trainings. IP judges' English skills are relatively higher as well.

Victor Xue:	In your opinion, is there any problems about China IP protection?

Zhang: *China adopts a double-track mechanism to protect IP rights, which includes administrative protection and judicial protection. Industrial and Commercial Agency's raid is the most powerful administrative action among the administrative measures. Every year, the AIC has around 30,000 IP cases, and most of them are trademark cases. On the other hand, the number indicates that Chinese companies are paying more attention to their IP rights during the economic development, and the companies complains more and more to the administrative agencies. However, IP rights is a kind of private right, and the government should not involve too much in protecting private rights, in particular for the patent cases. I'm also thinking about this issue recently.*

After all, China only has 20 years IP experience, so the existence of certain deficiencies is inevitable. The biggest issue in China is that IP protection is not only related to legal issues, but also the foreign trade and political issues. We must resolve this problem in the future. Also, there are rooms for the improvement on the mode of IP trial. Mr. Zhang's article states that according to the rules of Supreme People's Court, the cases are designated to the IP tribunal or administrative tribunal of Beijing No1 Intermediate People's Court based on whether the cases relate to civil disputes. And the parties can appeal the case to the corresponding tribunals of Beijing High People's Court or Supreme People's Court. The problem is that the IP tribunal and Administrative tribunal have big difference in terms of understanding of the cases, the trial method, and even the way how to draft judgment. Further, the adjudicating standards are not uniform in the two kinds of tribunals. In my opinion, all the cases should be handled by the same kind of tribunal, which is also a voice from IP practitioners and professionals. The jurisdiction over IP civil cases and IP criminal cases is not uniform. For example, according to the relevant rules form Supreme People's court, generally, the IP civil trial should be decided by the Intermediate People's Courts or certain local people's courts designated by High People's Court, while the IP criminal trials are basically decided by the local district people's courts. Due to the inconsistence of the jurisdiction standard, sometimes. the judgments on the civil case and the criminal case caused by the same conduct are inconsistent.

It is very difficult to train IP judges. A court clerk need to work 3 years to be promoted to an assistant judge. Further promotion takes more time and is even more difficult. However, the courts are undergoing serious talent drain, such as my leaving (laugh).

[Mr. Zhang's article supplements that the current judges are not sufficient to handle the increasing number of IP cases, though the Beijing No 1 Intermediate People's Court readjusted judges of IP tribunal. In addition, with the increase of IP cases, the IP cases become more complicated and difficult, which imposes higher requirements on IP judges. From the training cycle of IP judge, at least, the court need three years to train a qualified IP judge from a court clerk or a judge from other fields.]

During the IP litigation, foreign parties may raise certain unreasonable requests and conduct certain stupid actions, because they are not aware of China judicial system or evidence rules. For example, in an IP infringement case regarding an oil information system, the foreign attorney modified and standardized the evidence collected from the internet, put red circles or punctuations on the evidence, which destroyed the authenticity and value of proof of the evidence. The foreign parties should try to understand the Chinese legal culture and comply with it.

Victor Xue: You mentioned that sometimes foreign parties might raise certain unreasonable requests. Would you please give us an example?

Zhang: *Let's use the Viagra trademark case for example. The plaintiff Pfizer claimed that "Viagra" was the famous unregistered trademark, but did not obtain the court's support. Meanwhile, Pfizer also presented two claims that (1) the defendant should guarantee no further infringement will* *occur; and (2) the defendant should apologize to Pfizer. The apology is a kind of relief for personal rights. Since the trademark right does not have such personal right element, it is not appropriate to claim or grant such a relief. Therefore, the court denied Pfizer's request.*

Victor Xue: The current issued Anti-Monopoly Law mentions IP monopoly issue. What is your opinion on it?

Zhang: *The Anti-Monopoly Law is a law of general principle. The detailed rules relating to IP misuse and monopoly will be defined later. It is not practical to discuss this issue currently.*

Victor Xue: What is the effect of precedent value of cases in China?

Zhang: *First, in China, earlier cases do not have binding effect on the subsequent cases. However, it is obvious that decisions from the higher courts have significant influence on the lower courts' decisions. The Supreme People's Court's guiding cases and certain IP cases decided by high-quality courts also have actual influence on the lower court's decisions. In practice, the court system's attitude is to encourage such positive influence. As for the foreign decisions, we only use them as references. The foreign decisions can not guide China court's practice, or be used as evidence in the court.*

Victor Xue: Finally, could you talk about the practical use of doctrine of equivalents in Chinese courts?

Zhang: *Doctrine of equivalents was used in deciding patent cases. The concept derived from US, and is mainly adopted in mechanical and chemical cases. Based on my understanding, doctrine of equivalents is a principle to determine infringement rather than a principle to limit the scope of the patent rights, which is commonly recognized in Chinese legal community.*

Yang Meng

Time and Place:	August 2007 Beijing
Attendees:	Victor Xue, IP author and scholar Wen Xu, currently a law student of Northwestern University Law School Ms. Meng, director of Department of Policy and Legal Affairs of PRC General Administration of Customs.

Meng Yang graduated from Renmin University in Beijing, worked at China customs since. Director General Meng is one of the top experts in enforcing IP rights in China. She was at front-line in many high profile cases. She represented China Customs in many international negotiation, got numerous awards for stopping counterfeit products at China Customs.

The below interview was originally conducted in Chinese and the English translation was unedited from the original interview.

Victor Xue:	As a leader of department in General Administration of Customs, the most important department on the front of IP border protection, could you please talk about the IP protection of Chinese Customs?

Meng: *Our conversation today is a private talk between friends, which should not be regarded as an official statement on behalf of General Administration of Customs.*

According to our statistics, the IP border protection was improved in 2006, and China Customs successfully strengthened its actions against the import/export of IP infringing products. In a year, China Customs blocked 2,475 sets of IP infringing products, and seized about one hundred million infringing items which is worth more than two hundred million Yuan.

Our achievement is quite obvious and fruitful. The number of seized products in 2006 (2,475 sets) is twice more than the number in 2005. Not only the large shipment of products was inspected, we also started the inspection on small posts, and sometimes our Customs official checked one or two small shipments. Customs officials did lots of efforts on the border IP protection. Our achievement was not only contributed by the Customs official inspectors, but also contributed by the vertical leading structure of China Customs which guaranteed the efficiency of border IP protection.

Victor Xue: Is the Customs' border protection available and effective on all IP rights, such as patent, copyright an trademark?

Meng: *Frankly speaking, we have not done much inspection and seizure regarding patent and copyright cases, because we are under a tremendous pressure to open the containers in front of the purchasers and the distributors. The cases relating to patent and copyright are more complex than trademark cases, therefore, it is not easy for our on-site Customs officials to determine whether the goods infringe the patent or copyright. We have done few cases of design patents. For the invention patents, only if we are provided very detailed information and training, as well as very accurate clues, we might do the on-site inspection.*

Normally trademark case is more straightforward, and we have done a lot of inspection and seizure. Lots of trademark right owners expressed their appreciation to China Customs.

Victor Xue: Considering the overall IP protection as a whole, how important the border IP protection is?

Meng: *I'd like to talk about my personal opinion. In China, the IP protection authorities are separated into different government departments, including AIC, Copyright Bureau, Patent Office, SIPO, Bureau of Quality and Technical Supervision, Courts and General Administration of Customs. The interaction among governing authorities increases the cost of IP protection. For the border IP protection, all IP related matters are governed by the Customs, which I believe is an effective and efficient structure.*

Compared with the other IP protection departments, the IP border protection can reduce the right holders' cost, and it is easy for the right holders to enforce their rights. Further, the quality of Customs officials team is relatively higher, and we keep a good cooperation and communication with the right holders. Meanwhile, all Customs in the world have close connections, for example, China Customs and EU Customs co-hosted certain forums to discuss inspection and experiences in the past few years. The China Customs officials are willing to discuss and learn the advanced experience from other overseas Customs, as a consequence, the quality and capacity of our work have been improving.

Victor Xue:	Certain foreign media always reported that China was the source of counterfeiting products. How do you think about this?

Meng: *Such kind of reports were extremely irresponsible and the reporters had not had any idea of the IP border protection situation in China.*

The annual value of the global IP infringing products is around USD five hundred billion dollars which accounts for 5-7% of the global trade value in the world. In 2003, China exported USD92.47 billion products to America, and around USD60 million products were suspected of IP infringing and seized by the US Customs, which accounts for 0.06% of the whole export value.

This statistics indicated that the ratio of the IP infringing exportation to the whole exportation is much lower than the average global level. And the China Customs IP border protection is in the first tier among other Customs in the world.

In addition, China is the only country in the world which inspects and checks the exportation out of the country. The inspection rate is around 0.2% in average, and it is even higher during certain special period. Considering China's whole trading (export) value, counterfeiting products from China is not at a high percentage. The statement of certain foreign medias, 70% counterfeit are from China, has no ground. When I attended some conferences in America, sometimes I would talk about this issue. I asked the foreign

86

governmental officials to provide certain statistics or relevant information which could support such a statement, and we wished to solve the counterfeiting problem based on the information they provided. However, I never received any supporting statistics information or data. It is irresponsible to keep providing such misleading information to the public without any supporting evidence. The Chinese Customs officials received lots of blames for which they were not deserved.

Victor Xue:	What is your strategy to face or respond the blames or accusation overseas?

Meng: *From a general perspective, IP protection directly relates to the Country's economic strength. When I attended a WIPO conference this year, some undeveloped African countries unexpectedly accused China's counterfeiting issue, I responded and rebutted immediately. Their blame had no basis and it was just an intention to circulate misleading information against China. One of my deepest impressions is that when you have to deal with people from developed countries you should be proactive. Your wonderful achievements could be meaningless, if you do not communicate them openly and could not convince the foreigners to understand what China Customs has done and are doing. Otherwise, foreigners continue to be misled by the untruthful information and continue to assume that China Customs does not perform well.*

From an outside point of view, many of our officials are able to make presentations overseas in English fluently, so we have received positive recognition of our ability and performance, as well as China's effort on its global responsibility.

From an inside point of view, we should focus on developing our economy first. With the rising economy, the counterfeit problem will be less and the sales of the authentic products will increase. Second, IP education is a key issue to deter IP infringement. We should educate the relevant publics, enterprises and institutes, in order to avoid the "innocent" infringement" or "innocent" crime of IP rights. The IP education should be on a long-term basis and I believe it will be a successful and effective way to solve the IP infringement problem in China. In addition to the above mentioned, China Customs' IP protection achievement is well recognized domestically, which was witnessed by many awards we received. China Customs has been open minded and cooperated closely with right owners. We will keep our efforts on the IP border protection based on the achievements we have made.

Victor Xue:	Could you talk about the steps the Customs has taken, in terms of the education issue?

Meng: *There are various levels of education. For the Customs, we should first educate the exporters and distributors who have direct connection with the counterfeiting products, as well as small and medium manufacturers. We have begun the education several years ago and achieved pretty good results. Once the enterprises or distributors are aware of the risks of exporting counterfeits, they will balance whether it is worth to take the risks. They are business people and they will not take unprofitable risks. As a consequence, we will decrease the possibility of "innocent" infringement. With in depth investigations, we discover that sometimes the behind-the-scene master minds are foreigners who are purchasers of the counterfeits. Unfortunately, due to regulatory limitation, we are not able to chase the source of the counterfeit goods overseas. . Therefore, what we can do is to reduce the possible counterfeit trade by educating the exporters and distributors.*

Victor Xue:	Which kind of IP rights are infringed most seriously?

Meng: *Personally, I think it should be the copyright. Because it is easy to infringe others' copyright and the demand of copyright infringing products is really high.*

Victor Xue:	With respect to the IP border Protection by criminal measures, China Customs and Ministry of Public Security jointly issued a MOU last year. How about the enforcement of the MOU?

Meng: *We keep a good cooperation with Ministry of Public Security. But there is a main discrepancy regarding the determination of the value involved in the case, so we actually do not transfer many cases to Ministry of Public Security. I'd like to* mention the differences of IP protection between China and US. US does not have criminal liability for IP infringement, but requests China to set up criminal liability of IP infringement. It is unfair to request China to perform additional obligation beyond what has been imposed by TRIPs under the WTO framework.

Victor Xue:	Does the China Custom's border IP protection mainly rely on the right holders' complaint? Does Customs have certain measures by itself?

Meng: *IP owner's complaint is one of the means for initiating our inspection which is called passive protection.*

China Customs has a proactive protection measure by operating its own risk monitoring and control system which contains black lists and other analyses to lock down targets. For example, if the system finds an exportation of shoes to a small country in Africa, where the shipment has a large quantity and the unit price is very low, then our risk monitoring and control system will send an alarm. Then we will do the inspection and ascertain whether there is any infringing issue. China Customs has already successfully used such system for a while. Further, a black list system will be available throughout the country by network, so that each customs at different ports of entry will be able to analyze the information in a universal and consistent way. For example, if one distributor once infringed, it will be closely monitored even if the port of entry has been changed.

Victor Xue:	During the IP border protection, does the Customs encounter any special difficulties?

Meng: *Difficulties exist all the time. Now the counterfeiting activities are becoming more and more undercover. The infringers falsely declare the goods, mix or separate the shipping products, change different packaging, use similar trademarks, and etc. It is increasingly difficult for the Customs to check and find out the infringing products. However, the worst scenario is that some IP owners do not collaborate with us, and sometimes they will settle the case with the infringer and disregard the fact that the goods are seized by the Customs. For example, once we actively seized* *some counterfeit products, and the IP owners certified those products were counterfeits. However, the IP owner realized that the quality of the counterfeiting products were pretty good, and then the IP owner made an OEM contract with the counterfeiter. In the middle of the Customs proceeding, the IP owners provided an authorization of such exportation and asked Customs to release these counterfeiting products out of Chinese border. The Customs officials worked really hard to help IP owners stop the infringing products from the border, but finally the infringing products became authorized products. It frustrates the Customer officials and gives them little confidence on proactive protection, and also indicates/reflects that the right owners think little about its IP rights. They should have either notified the Customs that the seized goods were not infringing before the proceeding or after the completion of the proceeding, but not in the middle, as their sudden switch of position could discourage the Customs from protecting their rights proactively in future. ,IP owners should consider the situation as a whole rather than only focusing on short-term benefit.*

Victor Xue: Thank you for your time to take our interview.

Dr Zhi Yang

Time and Place:	10am August 22, 2007 @ Starbucks in Zhangjiang Pharma Valley, Shanghai
Attendees:	Zhi Yang, Founder, Chairman and Managing Partner, BioVeda China Fund
	Catherine Sun, Managing Partner, Foley & Lardner LLP Shanghai Office
	Victor Xue, IP author and scholar
	Harold Wegner, Professor, George Washington University Law School
	Wen Xu, currently a law student of Northwestern University Law School

Dr Yang has over twenty years of experience in the Life Sciences Industry in China and the U.S. as a venture capital investor, senior management executive, entrepreneur and scientific inventor. As a venture capitalist, in 2005 Dr. Yang formed BioVeda China Fund, which is the first international Life Science and Healthcare investment firm in China. Dr. Yang has raised capital from prominent Asian, European and U.S. international institutional, corporate and financial blue chip investors for his private growth stage Funds. Dr. Yang has developed a highly successful and diversified portfolio of primarily growth stage companies in the biopharmaceuticals, medical technology, healthcare services and industrial biotechnology sectors that include CITIC Pharmaceutical, Cathay Industrial Biotech, Ltd., Novast Pharmaceuticals, Nexchem Pharmaceuticals, NOD Pharmaceuticals, Ealong Biotech, and Stateview International (Aildenafil). Prior to founding BioVeda China Fund, Dr. Yang was Co-founder and General Partner of BioVeda Capital, a venture capital firm that invested in Asia and U.S. for which he created a successful portfolio with top performance compared with peers and bench mark. Among twelve investee companies, there are six exits (4 IPOs and 2 acquisitions). As a senior management executive, Dr. Yang was former Executive Vice President of business development of Sinogen International Ltd., which was created by H&Q Asia Pacific, as a vehicle to acquire biotech and pharmaceutical companies in China, and the vehicle for NASDAQ IPO. He spearheaded an

M&A group and acquired Shangdong Kexin Biotech, Beijing Hua-er-dun Vaccine Co. and Egen Corp., and was appointed as VP of sales and marketing in charge of over 150 sales people in Shanghai. Prior to Sinogen, Dr. Yang held senior scientific and management positions in both biotech and pharmaceutical companies, including Sinogen, Incyte Pharmaceuticals, Prolinx, Sandoz Pharmaceuticals, and Systemix. As an entrepreneur, Dr. Yang started and co-founded biotech businesses in both China and the U.S. including: Trans-Pacific Recombinant Technology (exit), BioChain Institute (exit), Crimson Pharmaceuticals, Genex BioScience, Biotech Core (exit), Sciprogene, and ScinoScience Partners.

Dr. Yang received his Masters and Ph.D. in Biochemistry and Molecular Biology from Harvard University. Dr. Yang was ranked #1 among all graduate students in the class of 1982 of the Chinese Academy of Medical Sciences; and among the first group of 21 students, selected from several thousand, to study in the U.S. in 1982 with the CUSBEA (China-U.S. Biological Science Education Association) program. Dr. Yang is the principal inventor of more than 10 U.S. and international patents, and prior to joining industry, was a Senior Associate Fellow and faculty member at Rockefeller University. Dr. Yang is an Advisor to the China Health & Medical Development Foundation under the Ministry of Health (Beijing, China).

Dr. Yang is Chairman of the Board of CITIC Pharmaceutical, Novast Pharmaceuticals, Nexchem Pharmaceuticals, and StateView International, and is a member of the Board of Directors of Cathay Industrial Biotech.

Dr. Yang is the founder, Chairman and Managing Partner of BioVeda China Fund. As a seasoned investor and leading expert in China's life science sector, Dr. Yang has successfully consummated and exit a number of high profile deals. BioVeda China Fund is focused exclusively on the Life Sciences and Healthcare industries in China. His fund primarily targets the following sectors:

- Biopharmaceuticals and Biotechnology
- Traditional Chinese Medicine
- Medical Technology
- Healthcare Services (hospitals, clinics, IT systems)
- Pharmaceutical & Medtech logistics & distribution
- Industrial Biotechnology ("greentech")
- Agricultural Biotechnology
- Nutraceuticals

Intro:	Catherine introduced our program to Dr. Yang and emphasized that our final neutral report was aiming to provide "authentic" information regarding China IP, as well as to provide an IP communication channel between China and the outside world. Prof. Wegner supplemented that the significance of this program was not only to provide accurate information regarding China IP practice to the mainstream American IP society, but also to convey various opinions to the new generation of Chinese leaders. Dr. Yang agreed and believed that IP should be part of the core assets of a company. In valuating a company, Dr. Yang's working motto is that "No IP – no value". In this regard, many Chinese business people can not accept the concept yet, supplemented by Dr. Yang.

Dr. Yang: *I will share a story with you first. Fifteen years ago, Microsoft sued a small Beijing-based company for copyright piracy. Due to lack of litigation experience, the CEO of the small company decided to defend in the trial by himself. During his closing statement, the CEO told the Court emotionally "I was a student of Tsinghua University and I liked jogging. Everyday I ran through the Summer Palace which was stolen, robbed and destroyed by the Anglo-French allied armies. You, the foreigners taught me that stealing was neither wrong nor criminal. Now, you are suing me for copyright infringement which is absolutely unacceptable." The audiences in the Court all stood up and applauded for him. Being part of the benefits from this lawsuit, the small company became famous after the case. The story showed the sentiment of Chinese toward foreigners.*

Dr. Yang: *Let's recount the historical development of Chinese pharmaceutical industry. Before 1992, drugs were not patentable in China, because during that period, the government believed that the healthcare was not just a business but also related to people's welfare. Thus, China should not provide excusive rights to drugs and should allow the citizens freely benefit from the new drugs developed in the world. With the revision of the Chinese Patent Law effective on January 1st, 1993, drugs could be patentable, such an attitude has been changing ever since. The pharmaceutical industry in China underwent the following three stages:*

1. Umbrella protection stage, when the whole domestic industry freely benefitted from the global development;

2. Improvement stage, when the domestic industry had its own innovation instead of pure replication; and

3. Innovation stage: when fundamental innovation can lead a company to the first tier in the industry.

Dr. Yang: *With the industrial development, the Chinese returnees can also be classified into three groups.*

1. Liars/ losers/ low quality returnees;

2. Imitators/ initial inventors/ professionals with advanced technologies; and

3. Inventors/ Innovators/ leaders/ good quality returnees.

Wegner: *For the third wave of returnees, they can compete with the local American citizens if they choose to stay in the United States. However, they volunteered to come back to China.*

Dr. Yang: *The third group / wave is important in leading China into innovation stage. Catherine is a good example of the third wave of returnees in that she is experienced with American and Chinese legal practices. As a biotech capital venture investment professional, I never invested into a company without any IP assets. In China, the "solid" condition is good enough, but there is a lot of room to improve for "soft" conditions.*

Wegner: *First there should be enough capable R&D professionals; second the professionals should be aware of that their researches relate to intellectual property issues; third the professionals should have certain knowledge on the patent and international patent system in order to protect their invention on a worldwide basis.*

Dr. Yang: *Compared with the situation in the United States, the innovation cost in China is relatively low. Nowadays, the research professionals have a general idea of intellectual property, and pay certain attention to the Chinese patent filings. However, they do very few international filings, because the international filing cost is relatively high to the Chinese patent owners. Then how should we encourage the*

Chinese inventors in making international patent filings? I have a creative idea which is still priliminary. I plan to establish an intellectual property fund to support the international patent filings of certain biotech technology or patent which has a good potential.

Wegner: The reason why an inventor does not want to cooperate with business person to file international patent is that: normally the inventor wants to control everything in the inventing process. So the inventor does not want to involve the business people to co-own the patent with them.

Wegner: The R&D professionals can file the Chinese patent first and try to get certain financial support during the next 12 months. The inventors could invite certain foundation, companies or business people to review and evaluate their invention confidentially. Before the expiration of the priority date, the inventors may have collected enough finance to continue its international patent filings, even the finance of further research and development.

Dr. Yang: Thank you for sharing the information. I am trying to establish certain entity that gathers the venture capitalists, patent professionals, experts and business persons to set up such an IP foundation.

Dr. Xue: The Stanford University patent licensing center is the most successful patent licensing center in the world. The center profited from its participation in the development of Google.com.

Wegner: Patent rights and patent collaboration is really important for the pharmaceutical industry. The exclusive right of certain patent is sometimes crucial to a pharmaceutical company. Unlike the companies in other industry, such as Microsoft, which achieved success with its entire patent portfolio, the pharmaceutical companies might succeed with only one patent.

Ms. Sun: What kind of companies BioVeda may choose to invest, including both private companies and state owned companies?

Dr. Yang: *Our targets include private companies and state owned companies. As the investment market in biotech just began, we did not have much challenge till now. Actually, 80% of target companies are private companies. At the current stage, some profitable companies can be easily listed in the public stock market and have a good return of investment, even there is no much innovation in the companies. Until now, no company in China can have a high profit margin solely relying on its intellectual property.*

The biotech industry is competitive. First, the generic drugs can not go through the clinical trials, because the companies producing generic drugs are afraid of being sued by giant pharmaceutical companies. Actually, only a few of the biotech companies are profitable, and a successful company need the talented technical professionals, marketing and sales persons. Second, compared with the past, the American and European companies began to launch their newly developed drugs into China market. They all face the challenges.

Wegner: *How about the German investment in China?*

Dr. Yang: *German companies are very friendly to China and they have the most investment in China biotech industry. German companies have a good relationship with China government in different levels.*

> **Ms. Sun:** I heard that Germans like the people from Shandong Province, because they all love beers. (laugh)

Dr. Yang: *I want to emphasize the importance of IP for a chemical and biotech company. Let's take the Vitamin C for example first. In the mid of 1980s, the Chinese technical persons developed a new producing process of Vitamin C. Due to the cost-saving of the new process, the new process occupied the market rapidly. Roche, the patent right owner of Vitamin C, was significantly impacted by the Chinese new technology. However, the Chinese inventor did not have the patent right of Vitamin C, eventually the Chinese inventor had to license Roche to use the new process at a really low royalty fees.*

> *One example of BioVeda's investment, we invested into the leading company, Cathay, in biotech industry, because we believed the company has an outstanding IP portfolio and a promising future. Some other examples also illustrate the importance of IP, such as we invested in companies that produce vaccines for flu and rabies, as well as biofuels.*

Wegner: *How to educate the leaders of Chinese companies to have a better understanding of intellectual property?*

Dr. Yang: *It is a very complicated issue. There are mainly two generations of business leaders in China now. The older generation does not have much IP knowledge but they do understand the importance of intellectual property. The young generation has some IP knowledge but they thought they knew everything, which is very risky.*

Dr. Xue: Do you invest to a profitable company whose IP portfolio is not well managed?

Dr. Yang: *It is really important to conduct an IP due diligence on the target company at an early stage, which discloses the valuable IP assets and disadvantages of IP of a company. If we find the target company is manufacturing Viagra, we will remove this generic drug from the company's asset list, and only consider the good IP assets.*

Ms. Sun: How do you deal with the risk of potential litigation in your invested company? Are you afraid of "buying" a lawsuit?

Dr. Yang: *It is on a case by case basis. Let's take Cathay for example. It is important to conduct the IP due diligence of the target company, and identify the potential disputes in its IP portfolio. Sometimes it is a big challenge, because certain traditional companies treat the patent information as confidential information and do not want to disclose to the potential investors. It seems that their technologies are really good and profitable. Based on my previous experience, the private companies is much easier to cooperate than the state owned companies on IP issues.*

Next month, one company invested by us will be listed in Shenzhen Stock Exchange. The company has two kinds of new good drugs, one for rabies and one for flu. These two kinds of drugs were awarded gold medal in the life science field and have lots of potential in the future. Many venture capitals interested in investing the company and the company finally chose BioVeda. The company's expectation is more than money. I'm an expert in the biotech industry and we discussed the further development of the drugs and the company.

BioVeda China Fund is the first international venture capital aiming at the biotech industry. Lots of people thought I was crazy in investing on China biotech industry because it was too risky. Although the China biotech industry is not competitive right now, I believe we will have certain progress three years later. There are too many "crazy" elements in the biotech industry and in China.

Ms. Sun:	Who are the investors of BioVeda?

Dr. Yang: *Our investors include HBM BioVentures, World Bank, IFC, Temasek Holdings, private corporations, worldwide individual investors and etc.*

Wegner: *How is the possibility to cooperate with German and Japanese investment?*

Dr. Yang: *We already have certain cooperation, but the cooperation is mainly on the licensing aspect after the Chinese companies were listed. There is a special relationship between China and Japan. But they are business people, once they need the investment and have no choice of the source of the investment, it does not matter. However, if they have a choice between the American investment and the Japanese investment, they will definitely choose the American investment. Honestly speaking, the old generations still care this issue.*

Ms. Sun:	Compared with the beginning of your business, is the business becoming easier and better now?

Dr. Yang: *The Pudong government almost regarded us as a local "hero", because we assisted the government earned two million US dollars in a short period. (Laugh) Here is the story. I believed that Cathay will have a promising future, so I introduced Cathay to the Pudong government. If the government could invest into Cathay, when Cathay's products are launched in the market, the investment would be really valuable. The government showed its interest on the investment and promised to invest two million US dollars. But it is unexpected that the government further discovered that it can only invest in the Chinese currency and need three months to exchange the Chinese currency into US dollars if necessary. I agreed with the government proposal and tried to help Pudong government find certain loan, in order to invest the two million dollars on time. However, almost all financial institutions charge 15% to 20% interest for a 3-month loan of two million US dollars. Finally, a German company lent the government two million US dollars without charging any interest, with the aim to build a good relationship with the government. Three months later, when I contacted the government for the currency exchange issue, I was informed that the government needed six more months to exchange the dollars due to certain unexpected complication. I felt disappointed, but soon I realized that maybe the government can sell the shares of its investment to the German company. The deal was successfully done and the Pudong government was really happy with the outcome. Because Cathay had doubled its value in these three months, and Pudong government earned two million US dollars without using its own money. It well illustrated a Chinese proverb that "trap a wolf with bared hands". The Pudong government was excited with its first taste of capital.*

Another story is about the oral insulin. A company focusing on the research of oral treatment of hypoglycemia had obtained enough clinical trial data on animals. Then the company contacted me and hoped that we can provide the finance for the development of the drugs. In the pharmaceutical field, investment solely on technology is really unpredictable and risky. Therefore, although I was interested in investing his project, I need some human clinical trial data in addition to the data from animals. It surprised me that only several days later the founder of the company came back with human clinical trial data. When I asked where he got the human clinical data, he frankly admitted that the data was obtained from the trial on himself and his dad. It is not an advisable way to provide the data, but their spirit really impressed me. So I decided to invest fifty thousand US dollars into the company first, in order to help them go through the human clinical trial. It is only an issue of fifty thousand dollars. If the human clinical trial is successful, I will keep investing in the company. This story has a satisfactory ending.

Wegner: With respect to the human clinical trial, it is apparent that the cost in China is much lower than the cost in U.S. But certain companies have the concern that whether the test result in China can be recognized and accepted by the American FDA.

Dr. Yang: The China market is important to each pharmaceutical company and I will try to convince the Chinese pharmaceutical companies to conduct the clinical trials in China. Can you imagine that during the past 4 years, we spent 500 million Yuan on the second phases clinical trial of two drugs. Eli Lily and other big pharmaceutical companies are paying close attention on our investment and they probably will purchase the drugs when the drugs pass the third phase of test. It will be a win-win business.

After the interview, Dr. Yang showed us his office and team at Phama Valley, and Dr. Xue presented one of his patent books to Dr. Yang.

Alex An

Time and Place:	September 14th, 2010 9:00am via conference call at Foley & Lardner's Shanghai Office
Attendees:	Alex An, CEO of JK Sucralose Catherine Sun, Managing Partner, Foley & Lardner LLP Shanghai Office Vanessa XU, Legal Assistant, Foley & Lardner LLP Shanghai Office

Alex AN (Lijun AN) is the CEO of JK Sucralose Inc. JK Sucralose Inc. is the largest professional sucralose manufacturer in China and the second largest in the world. JK Sucralose Inc. is:

- *The only enterprise in China that participated in the US ITC intellectual property investigation on its own initiative; it has been affirmed that JK Sucralose is non-infringing*
- *The only sucralose manufacturer in China with 4,000 MT long-term designed annual capacity;*
- *The only enterprise in China with 100,000-grade standard GMP workshop;*
- *The only sucralose enterprise in China that established professional direct sales companies in the US and Europe;*
- *One of the major initiators to obtain a national standard for sucralose;*
- *The only sucralose enterprise that owns proprietary intellectual property rights and has applied for 7 patents in China and 4 patents in the US.*

Mr. An graduated from Zhangzhou Teachers Colleague in 1983, after spending 15 years in the Science & Technology Committee under the City of Shijiazhuang, he resigned his official role and started to do business. He first worked as CEO & General Manager for Shijiazhuang Guangfu Food Additive Co., Ltd. for 6 years, and then joined Beijing Fubai Shide Technology Co., Ltd. as CEO for 3 years. In Oct. 2006, Tate & Lyle, a US Sweetener manufacturing company raised ITC 337 investigation to a number of Chinese companies. Mr. An joined JK Sucralose Inc. as CEO at this critical and difficult moment. Under his leadership, JK Sucralose Inc. initiatively Intervened in the ITC 337 investigation, after two years' time and cost of 20Million RMB, JK Sucralose Inc. won the case overwhelmingly.

On April 7th, 2007, a leading Sucralose Company, Tate & Lyle filed a 337 investigation against three Chinese manufactures as well as US distributors, claiming the infringement of patent process for producing sucralose, a zero-calorie artificial sweetener. Although JK Sucralose was not listed as a defendant in the investigation, Mr. Alex An, the CEO of JK Sucralose, decided to voluntarily join into the investigation. Finally, JK Sucralose won the landmark case and was extensively reported by media for its courageous story. We met Alex in summer 2009 at a SAIC conference where Catherine was the VIP speaker on China brands going overseas. Alex , who was frequently interviewed by media in China, kindly agreed to participate our interview. During Tianjin meeting, Alex confidently claimed only proactively participating a US patent litigation, you could turn your litigation cost into investment.

Below interview was originally conducted in Chinese and the English translation was unedited from the original interview.

Ms. Sun:	Only a few Chinese companies are not afraid of being involved in any US litigation or 337 investigation, and fewer could reach the final victory. What was your thought after JK winning the 337 case?

Alex An:	*In fact, it is the first case that a Chinese company voluntarily defended in a 337 investigation even it was not listed as a respondent. I think we have a different perspective with other companies. In my opinion, when a Chinese company expands into the overseas market, such as US market, it will obviously share or take certain portion of the foreign market. The foreign companies will treat the new Chinese company as a competitor, and therefore will try any means to prevent the Chinese company's expansion in the relevant market. Proactive actions are always better than the passive defenses.*

Ms. Sun:	Once a lawsuit is filed in the United States, most Chinese parties will choose to settle the case as soon as possible, but you decided to be aggressive and fight back on your own initiative. How did such a decision come into your mind?

Alex An:	*Actually, it is a matter of mentality. The money spent on the defense of a lawsuit is deemed as costs, while the money spent*

on proactive action is deemed as an investment. We should get in front of the issue, which will offer you more leverage and more likelihood of success during the litigation. It is not a matter of money but a matter of how to prepare. The key issue in our mind is that we should treat the lawsuit to be an investment.

Ms. Sun: In your case, JK Sucralose actually was a respondent. Even for a respondent, do you agree that it is still better to take proactive actions?

Alex An: *Early or late is a relative concept. It is never too late for a respondent to prepare in advance. You should keep the proactive concept in mind, and good preparation may help you turn round the situation and even turn a likely defeat into a victory. Being prepared in front of the issue provides you with the initiative for the subsequent work.*

Ms. Sun: At the beginning, was your idea supported by the management, such as the board of directors?

Alex An: *Most of them did not agree with me at the beginning. Then I explained the 337 investigation procedure to my colleagues and analyzed our current situation. Only three Chinese companies were listed as respondents by Tate & Lyle initially, and we became the fourth who voluntarily joined. According to the US law, if the ITC issues a general exclusion order against the product, JK's same product can not be imported into the territory of United States and JK may lose the US market. On the other hand, if the named Chinese respondents win the case, the US consumers will prefer to purchase the products from the named respondents than JK's because the products of the named respondents are proved to be non-infringing by the court. Considering the above two factors, JK decided to voluntarily join this 337 investigation. Before the 337 investigation, we had started to prepare filing a lawsuit before the federal district court. Due to this unexpected 337 investigation, we started to consider participating it. Before joining the 337 investigation, we spent nearly one month and had a dozen of conference calls with US lawyers to analyze the infringement issues. Finally we cleared infringement issue of three patents by our products. For its fourth patent, it might relate to our producing process, but the patent would* *expire on September 2007. We joined the 337 investigation in July 2007, so we just need to ensure that our products not enter into US market before September 2007. For its fifth patent, it was arguable whether we infringed the patent. The fifth patent expired on July 2009, and we predicted that the 337 decision would be issued around the beginning of 2009. So even if we lost the case, the excusive order would only block us from the US market for a few months.*

The last expiring date of one of the five patents is in 2023. Based on the facts and comprehensive analysis above, I convinced the management to agree to join the 337 investigation.

Ms. Sun:	During the long term cooperation with foreign law firms, do you feel any cultural or language barrier between a Chinese company and the foreign lawyers? Can these lawyers exactly understand your strategy of the case?

Alex An: *No, they did not understand at the very beginning that why we voluntarily chose to join the 337 investigation. Everybody knows that defending a 337 case will cost millions of dollars. And actually, the complainant can not find any public information of our company before we voluntarily joined the 337 investigation. We do not want to become a target before we are ready. We voluntarily joined the 337 investigation, because we were prepared and we wanted to take the initiative.*

Ms. Sun:	Had your company been prepared before the 337 action?

Alex An: *Yes, definitely. I believe the battle is inevitable, because we are taking the Complainant, our US competitor's market share.*

Ms. Sun:	Did you join any respondent group or cooperate with other respondents against the complainant in the investigation?

Alex An: *Actually, we did not. Because Tate & Lyle filed the 337 investigation in April, and our participation was approved by*

ITC on August 15. We were not able to keep the same timeline with other respondents, so we defended alone.

Ms. Sun:	How many times did you travel between China and US during this 337 investigation?

Alex An: *Not too much, only twice.*

Ms. Sun:	Did you involve in the deposition procedure during the investigation?

Alex An: *After being approval by the ITC on August 15, we disclosed all related materials (including the hard disks) to ITC before the end of August. We discussed the deposition location in September and finally chose Hong Kong. In October, four employees from JK went to Hong Kong to be deposed. And in the early of November, ITC sent about 8 persons to inspect our factory, including ITC staff attorney and lawyers from both sides. Totally, they took more than thirty samples and delivered the samples back to US for test. In February, our vice president and I testified in the ITC trial. I was the company representative and our vice president was an expert witness. The ITC finally decided that JK Sucralose did not infringe any patents of Tate & Lyle.*

We prepared very sufficiently for the case. I went to Washington DC 10 days prior to the trial. We simulated the hearing process several times and our attorneys listed thousands of possible questions.

Ms. Sun:	Is there any bilingual language speaker in your team?

Alex An: *Yes, we had our own translator when we simulated the hearing process. Also ITC officially assigned a Hong Kong citizen as the official translator agreed by both parties. Our own translator would correct us in case of any improper translations.*

Ms. Sun:	Do you think the language barrier will negatively influence a cross border lawsuit?

Alex An: *No, language barrier is not an issue. My greatest concern is the strategy. I need to take care of the direction rather than* details. In our case, I should decide whether to join the 337 investigation and how to defend if we were in.

| Ms. Sun: | How about the other respondents? Did they win? |

Alex An: *They also won the case. But during the two years, JK Sucralose was definitely the biggest winner. We grew up and became stronger, and now we are the second largest company in the relevant global market.*

| Ms. Sun: | I also see you more active in the media, as I have not heard from other respondents. |

Alex An: *I want to share our experience with Chinese companies who are afraid of suing in the US. On the other side, the positive media report has also helped our company to grow stronger and bigger.*

| Ms. Sun: | How long did you spend on this case? Did the case affect your business? |

Alex An: *About two years. The case did not affect my business much. Compared with other respondents, I have more time to concentrate on my business because I was very confident with the investigation.*

| Ms. Sun: | How about your customers? What was their attitude? |

Alex An: *They kept recognizing and accepting our products very well, because JK Sucralose was voluntarily involved into the 337 investigation.*

| Ms. Sun: | Did you need to explain more to your customers that your products did not infringe Tate & Lyle's patents? |

Alex An: *Yes, we did. We need to do some explanation, and our voluntary defense action further proved the non-infringement position. Our outside counsel sometimes needed to communicate with customers' counsel, and to clarify that we have done comprehensive research and investigation on Complainant's patents. We believed that we did not infringe their patent rights and now we were trying to prove our non-infringement in a legal process. Our customers trusted us.*

Ms. Sun:	How about the business development after the 337 case?

Alex An: *This year, our production could not keep up with the market demand. We predict that JK Sucralose will keep expanding our market in the next ten years. We have set up subsidiaries in US and EU, and currently we are establishing subsidiaries in Japan, Indian and south America.*

Ms. Sun:	Did the company consider setting up a legal department or an IP department in the company after this case?

Alex An: *Actually, I am now partially in charge of the legal department. Because we have only one type of products and we have structured the entire IP strategy before we set up this company. We take IP very seriously.*

Ms. Sun:	Will you plan to establish your patent portfolio in US, EU or Japan?

Alex An: *Yes, we are working on it. I think JK has obtained more patents in US than other Chinese companies in the industry. Compared with the electronic industry, a patent for chemical product or process is not easy to be conceived or granted. Until now, we have got two patents in US. The so-called patent pool is always in connection with the No. 1 leading enterprise or monopolistic company in an industry. As to the second or third ranked company, our main purpose is to avoid disputes.*

Ms. Sun:	Is Tate & Lyle still the No.1 leading company in the relevant industry? How big is their market share?

Alex An: *Yes, it is. Tate & Lyle is holding 70% of the relevant market. But we are the biggest in China.*

Ms. Sun:	Did the American financial crisis influence Tate & Lyle's market share?

Alex An: *No. Because the product is a really good man-made sugar processed from sucrose.*

Ms. Sun:	How did you start producing and selling such an artificial sugar product?

Alex An: *I did not involve into the R&D of the products, but I believed the products would have a good potential. I got into this industry in 2005 by trading sucralose. Then I cooperated with JK and became the major shareholder to control the company. Before joining JK, I had business with another company which was also sued in the same 337 case. During that time, the other company was sued before a Federal District Court in the United States, and I was involved and helped the company win. This federal case lasted nine months and finally the case was dismissed because Plaintiff lacked standing to sue. Therefore, I handled two different kinds of cases regarding sucralose in US. The strategies of the two cases were different, the strategy of the first case was to delay as much as possible and the strategy of the second case was to directly fight back.*

Ms. Sun:	How to ensure the patent quality of your company?

Alex An: *We engaged a big and experienced international patent firm for our patent prosecution matters in order to ensure the quality of our patent filings in the United States. So we are confident with the quality of our patents.*

The interview was ended when the ambitious businessman arrived the airport on his way to Nanjing. We agreed to keep the conversation ongoing by emails, phones or personal meetings should more questions arise.

Li Jianjun

Time and Place:	9am-11am April 2nd, 2010 Conference room of Shanghai Optimum Power and Environment Co Ltd, Shanghai
Attendees:	Mr. Li Jianjun, Chairman of Shanghai Optimum Power and Environment Co Ltd Ms. Yang. President of Shanghai Optimum Power and Environment Co Ltd Wen Xu, currently a law student of Northwestern University Law School Sally Shen, staff of Foley & Lardner LLP Shanghai Office

Jianjun LI is the director of Energy and Environment Investigation Development Center under Shanghai Academy of Sciences & Technology, an expert of Energy and Environment Protection Patent Exhibiting & Trading Center of China. He used to work as senior engineer and research director for SMDERI (Shanghai Marine Diesel Engine Research Institute). He also had the experience of working as assistant to county's head commissioner for one year, assigned by the organization department under Shanghai Municipal Government. He established several companies since 2001 and have been the general manager to these companies.

Mr. Li has been in the scientific research field for over 20 years, he focuses on the research and development concerning power protection, energy-saving and new energy technologies. His scientific achievements have won Shanghai Science & Technology Progress Award (2nd & 3rd Prizes); Shanghai Invention and Creation Award; China Science & Technology Progress Award (2nd Prize); No.6 most successful project in the sense of Science & Technology Achievement Transfer; most potential technology transaction elected by China International Industry Fair; Golden Bridge Prize by China Technology Market Association; Innovative Prize by China Non-governmental Enterprise Directors Association. He published a dozen of science & technology articles, has over 30 patent been/to be authorized both domestically and internationally.

Mr. Li current position is CEO of Shanghai Optimum Power and Environment Co., Ltd. He is a special entrepreneur, he is a perfect combination of precise technician and shrewd business man. He has rich experiences in leading Research & Development team in big science and technology enterprises, which results in his sharp judgment on product innovation. With the license fee for only one technology, he managed to rank as the second in terms of Shanghai Individual Intellectual Property Earning. He is the one who can turn idea into technology and to turn technology into profit. To him, Intellectual Property is the key to the success of a technology company. His motto is "We have to Fight to Survive".

Shanghai Optimum Power and Environment Co Ltd is one of the core units of Shanghai Science Academy Research and Development Center for Energy and Environment, researching and developing environment friendly products such as liquefied petroleum gas powered bikes, solar LED lights and so on. Mr. LI Jianjun, the Chairman has made profits from licensing the company's patent portfolio, which is still rare in China's small and medium size enterprises.

Wen Xu:	Can you introduce IP status in your company, especially data on your patents and patent licenses?

Li Jianjun: *Shanghai Optimum Power and Environment Co Ltd (SH OP&E) established in 2001 and has obtained 32 patents until now. We develop our own patent portfolio including design, utility model and invention to protect our new core technology. To that end, every patent plays a positive role. We do not file patent applications for the sake of filing for quantities. Instead, we are the type of enterprise focusing on innovation and research. For international patent applications, we have entered into Taiwan, Hong Kong, Egypt and other countries and regions via PCT. We once licensed one of our patents to a Taiwan company with a paid off royalty of RMB24.5 millions yuan (approximately 3.656 million US dollars) a year which was the second largest royalty recorded in Shanghai then. Our excellent management in patent made an exception-we were awarded the IPR Model Enterprise (second batch) by Shanghai Municipal Government, and enjoy the same honor and governmental support by the largest state owned enterprises such as Bao Steel, and Jinshan Petroleum and Chemical.*

Wen Xu:	How do you engage in patent development? Please introduce your R&D team.

Li Jianjun: *I always focus on R&D. From my perspective, only continued innovation can maintain the vitality of an enterprise. Revenue wise, our investment into R&D for the last ten years brings more than one hundred times of return. In 2008, a US PE Fund wanted to buy our 32 core patents as a package with 40 million US dollars and promised to help us to list on NASDQ with eight times P/E ratio, and also buy 25% shares of our company with eight million US dollars. Though the project was suspended due to economic crisis, it shows from one side that our company engaging in R&D and patent management is recognized by the market. Although our team is not large, everyone is talented and creative. We cooperate with each other and realize everybody's full potential. I had been a leader of 300 persons R&D team for a long time and engaged in thousands of R&D projects, which become an advantage in over-all planning and business. Therefore, the value proposition of our company is to continue innovation and stay ahead of the market.*

Wen Xu:	How your company conducts internal IPR management?

Li Jianjun: *My first patent application was filed in 1996. At that time, I thought that a good title of a patent would cover all products under that title. Nowadays, the patent royalty generates hundreds of times of our revenues. For the past decades, our company, especially me, have deep feeling to patents. From the beginning, I thought that patent was a title, so I spent a lot of time thinking of a good title. Later, I found that I was totally wrong. Patents have very strong technical discipline which should be handled by professionals. So, I started to cooperate with patent agents who helped to draft our patent applications. However, there were issues. Due to lack of familiarity of the technology, I feel the agents could not describe the inventive points appropriately and could not show the characteristics of the technology. Therefore, I started to draft patent applications on my own and often consult with SIPO's officials for patent wording. These years, I have gone to SIPO for more than 20 times. Such experience teaches me that granting a good patent is not easy. One error in selecting*

111

a word may cause design around or invalidated by competitors. After years of trying, our company involves patent agents during the entire process from technical discussions to making technical solutions, which enables the agents to understand the technology completely. We find such an approach is quite suitable to our company and receive very good results in practice.

Wen Xu:	How do you see China IP protection? After over 10 years dealing with IP, whether, do you think, China IP protection is making progress or moving in reverse?

Li Jianjun: *Of course, making progress, I should say enormous changes. The awareness to protect IP has been increased greatly nationwide. In 1996, the technical staff, like me, even had no sense to patent. Now, I lead a team to research IPR, develop IPR and establish our own IPR portfolio, and respect competitors' IPR. The progress and changes are very obvious.*

Wen Xu:	As I know that you have handled several patent cases, can you briefly talk about them?

Li Jianjun: *Strictly speaking, I have three patent cases: one is patent litigation and the other two are patent administrative enforcement. For patent litigation, we won the case. The opposing party was a state-owned enterprise and had no money to pay the damages. The court then decided to use opposing party's Hongqi (Red Flag) car to satisfy our damages. But we were awarded much higher damages. Friends of mine said to me such an enforcement was already pretty good. From side point of view, this case shows there is still big problem in China patent enforcement of judgment. Even you win, enforcement remains a big problem. This may be the reason why China enterprises are not willing to litigate patents.*

Wen Xu:	Based on foreign experience, when the losing party cannot satisfy the damages, the winning party could request to sell the losing party's shares to satisfy the damages.

Li Jianjun: *I have not thought this before. This may be a new idea. Thanks!*

The other two administrative enforcement cases do not involve damages. We lost one case between the two. The reason was very simple. To design around a patent is not difficult because every patent has defects. Take ballpoint pen for example, we researched and developed an automatic button head for ten years and filed for a patent. One of competitor who was familiar with the patent knew that it was profitable. He moved the automatic button from the head to the side which designed around our patent and did not constitute patent infringement. The SIPO after comparing the Claims 1-3 with his product, concluded there was no infringement, as they were not familiar with production process. For such a result, we are helpless.

Wen Xu:	Whether SIPO could be suggested that an individual similar to "people's juror" who is familiar with the technology, get involved in patent administrative cases?

Li Jianjun: *We had authentication and also expert opinions.*

Wen Xu:	What's your opinion about your company future IP strategy?

Li Jianjun: *Although we are a small company in its size, we actually have obtained positive result from IPR management, operation and commercialization. Almost, every core technology and its related patent receive over one hundred times of return, which allows us focus on technology innovation. We also understand that if our technology makes profit, counterfeit or copy is unavoidable. We shall always keep our technology more advanced over the competitors which is the only way to we can maximum our profits. Our special experience, when we develop a new technology which has been granted patent rights and commercialized, we would invite media to report it. For example, our one engine patent attracted more than 500 individuals or companies who wanted to cooperate with us, finally, we exclusively licensed our patent to a Taiwan enterprise with license fee of RMB24.5 millions yuan.*

Wen Xu:	When license term is expired, will you examine whether they still continue to use your patent?

Li Jianjun: *We are very satisfied with the income of this patented technology and we have developed the next generation or even the third generation of improved technology. The old technology has no advantage in the market, so it is not necessary for us to examine whether the licensee is still using the technology after the expiration of the license term. We see the issue not only from legal angle, but also from commercial and business relationship.*

I also want to share some lessons in internal management. Since we do not manufacture any products by ourselves, we usually found that the production partners counterfeited our technology which would be recognized by the market even during the technology research phase. After it happened several times later, I changed my strategy. I started to divide the key technology into several parts and deliver to different production partners to manufacture. Such as, the connection between different parts of the key technology would be controlled in our hand. It would be difficult for one production partner to counterfeit the entire technology, which protects our IPR better.

Wen Xu: In addition to patent protection, whether trade secret approach would also be adopted to protect the key technology?

Li Jianjun: *Patent is not enough to protect a core technology alone. A multilayer protection system would be more effective. Until now, our technical people have not violated any regulations, but the confidential agreements in all phases, technical barrier research, including patent and other information management have played its role respectively.*

Wen Xu: You have succeeded in patent commercialization. What kind of patent would be valuable in your view? Do you have any experience to share?

Li Jianjun: *I think, a good patented technology shall have one general characteristics – it provides a better and more effective technology without increasing cost. A friend once asked me that why no one was interested in his patented technology which could generate a huge energy saving effect only increasing a little cost. I told him that our technology could* *bring the same technical effect as yours without increasing any cost, why would others be interested at your technology. He was confused and said how I persuade customers to buy our technology if the inventive step was not complicated. In my opinion, an valuable patent could maximum the customer's interest. From patent protection perspective, if the competitors design around your complicated steps to get the same result, the competitors' technology would be more advanced. It is disappointing that the competitors obtain larger profit based on your technology. We once suffered from large economic lost that others made improvement based on our technology. I hope that other enterprises, inventors and patentees could be careful about this.*

Wen Xu:	Do you have any suggestion and experience to share when China IPR going global and facing intense international competition?

Li Jianjun: *Foreigners used to complain that we copied or counterfeited their technology. Currently, some famous multinational companies have copied or stolen domestic companies' technology. I once met a Japan motor company who had invited me to visit Japan for several times. Afterwards, I knew by coincidence that the Japanese company also wanted to develop a technology as mine and had spent a lot of money but failed finally. This proves that China technology is not always worse than foreigner's. Domestic companies shall be more confident. Besides, I met some foreign companies who wanted to know my technical secret in the name of cooperation by asking our detailed technology during negotiations. Later, I found that they just wanted to know my technical secrets without sincerity to cooperate. Often occurrence of such things naturally show that China IPR has started to be recognized by other countries. As long as China enterprises focus on R&D and learn from the developed IPR management experience carefully, there are more and more opportunities for China enterprises.*

Wen Xu:	Finally, can you briefly summarize your company and your IPR development experiences for the past ten years?

Li Jianjun: *From enterprise perspective, it is best that the CEO knows technology and cares about IPR. Nevertheless, IPR is very professional and need the whole enterprise involved. I divided IPR management into five parts: 1) strategy. We shall care about it from strategy; 2) tactics. It not only depends on our own study and understanding, but also shall borrow foreign developed experience, and moreover, rely on professionals; 3) system. IPR management is a system project which needs multi-departments to cooperate; 4) legal. Not only know China IP laws, but also know other countries' IP laws; 5) professional. Keep updating our knowledge and communicating with domestic and foreign professionals. The five items are complementary to each other.*

Li Fushan

Time and Place:	June 22, 2009 19:00 -20:30 Shenzhen Novotel Bauhinia Hotel
Attendees:	**Li Fushan**, Director of IP Department of Coship **Wen Xu**, currently a law student of Northwestern University Law School **Max Lin**, China Associate, Foley & Lardner LLP Shanghai Office

Fushan Li graduated from Southwest University of Political Science & Law. He worked first as a government official then joined Skyworth group. Now he is the head of Intellectual Property Department of Shenzhen Coship Electronics Co., Ltd. He was the founder of IP management system of Skyworth Group and Coship. He is good at the management of Enterprise IP and legal affairs. He is one of the founders of SZIPS (Shenzhen Enterprise IPR Manager Salon) as well as a researcher for IP Research Center under Southwest University of Political Science & Law.

Coship Electronics Co., Ltd. founded in 1994, is a listed well-known Hi-tech enterprise in China, specializing in R&D, manufacture and marketing of satellite/cable/terrestrial digital TV receivers, professional head-end IRD, IP STB (Set-Top Box), cable modem, GPS products, security products and LED displays. As the China's largest and one of global leading STB manufacturers, Coship provides global Pay TV operators with a variety of STBs worldwide deployed in Europe, Middle East, Asia, Australia, North America, South America and Africa.

With more than 4000 employees, 1050 of which are professional engineers, Coship has brought out various state-of-the-art products and technologies. Mr. Li Fushan is the Director of IP Department of Coship who provided some insights and reasons of the company's fast growth.

Below interview was originally conducted in Chinese and the English translation was unedited from the original interview.

Wen Xu:	What is the composition of your IP Department?

Li: *Totally, there are 10 persons in my department, among them, 7 persons engaged in patent prosecution, 3 persons focused on general IP law. IP department is an independent department which is overseen by Vice-president directly. The relatively high status of IP department in the corporate structure of COSHIP is due to business demand to IPR.*

Wen Xu: You have 10 people in your department, what issues do they handle on a daily basis?

Li: *Our work covers all issues related to IP. Specifically, our work can be divided into two parts: first, patent work, including patent prosecution, paper work relating to patent, patent invalidation, and patent management; second, risk management related to IPR, such as IPR risk in product development and marketing. In raw material supply procedure, we control IP risk from two aspects: one, avoid IP risk through specific clauses defined in the supplier agreement; second, identify suppliers with unfavorable IP record and try to exclude those suppliers.*

Wen Xu: Does IPR plays a role in domestic competition?

Li: *Frankly speaking, the importance of IPR has not been reflected in domestic competition. However, several kinds of IP issues have surfaced which realized the role of company's IP department. Actually, it's the role of company's IP department rather than the value of IPR itself that has been realized. Specifically, the IP issues in Coship business include customized development for customers who request for ownership of relevant IP, customers request to view source codes of certain products, and so on.*

Wen Xu: What's the likelihood that the management adopts the suggestion raised by IP department when IP department discovers certain IP risks in company's business decision making process?

Li: *It is more likely that the management will adopt our suggestion because our management takes the IPR seriously. Usually, Prior to making any important decisions, the management will take elements from legal, IP, technology and marketing departments into comprehensive consideration. From this perspective, the possibility that the suggestion put forwarded by IP department being adopted in its entirety is not high. However, due to the IP department's suggestion, the possibility that the management will take corresponding adjustment measures is very high. Based on our practical experience, with the formation of IP culture and awareness within the industry, the management has been increasingly influenced by IPR in their decision making. Additionally, more and more IP experience is exchanged and shared among companies in Shenzhen.*

Wen Xu: Does the *Chint vs Schneider* case influence the Coship IP strategy?

Li: *The damages award in **Chint vs Schneider** case was (and still is) the largest ever in China for patent infringement. Foreigners may believe that certain gray area in China's judiciary produced this decision. But based on my own understanding, we have to admit a few things: first, the judgment was made based on Chinese law; second, the entire procedure was open, transparent, and legitimate. As a landmark case in China, it influences enterprises physiologically and will not cause intensive IP battles among enterprises. To western friends, no matter from government, industry or legal, I hope that they can trust the law in China. China has been a society ruling by law since ancient time. China's law has its own characteristics. Do not think that China law always is full of politics or lots of gray areas exist in China law. If we have the same faith—respect law, then the laws in different countries should be respected. Bias toward one country can not be the excuse not to respect that country's law or give up to conduct any legal activity in that country.*

Wen Xu: What's the biggest problem in conducting IPR negotiations?

Li: *Different value proposition. After years' of negotiations, the parties are very familiar with each other, also respect each other, but just cannot close the deal. I summarized that the main reason for the failure is the different value proposition-where one company has a conflicting value proposition with the other company. Take the usual occurrence in IP area for example, one company has infringed other's IPR, the IPR owner claims a large compensation such as 50 million which may cause the bankruptcy of the company. It may be an issue relating to money (damage compensation), but not all about money. If it is pure money issue, agreement can be finally reached. Foreign companies like to take a simple approach but Chinese companies may be more difficult to read (such as they will bring up challenges faced, low profit margin). Most foreign companies regard these as an excuse and therefore would not listen or (accept). Therefore, many IP negotiations are at an impasse and cannot reach a deal, which does not help any side.*

Wen Xu: In order to meet international rules, Chinese companies passively not actively accept IPR. What do you think?

Li: *Absolutely, I am pretty sure. Our IP development is promoted by government. IP is only a tool.*

Wen Xu: Recently (for example, from 2005), how much progress has the Chinese companies made in IP negotiation involving foreign parties?

Li: *Three points: first, the "test water" period between Chinese party and foreign party is over; second, in recent years, from my understanding of Shenzhen IP circle, our skill and capability in IP has been improved greatly; third, western IPR owners have become more rational. I think, now is the best period for cooperation in IP.*

Wen Xu:	How do foreign companies select appropriate Chinese partners when they license technology?

Li: *Simply, it depends on whether the subject China company would hire foreign lawyers to participate the negotiation. If the Chinese company is willing to pay to hire foreign lawyers, it shows this company may be more into technology and have required sincerity.*

Wen Xu:	How Chinese companies select appropriate technology when they seek technology cooperation or technology transfer?

Li: *When we seek technology cooperation or technology transfer, we regard it as a purchase activity. Technology department is responsible for the technical assessment, while we (IP department) take risk and IP assessment. IP department will offer known license fees or royalties, in addition to a risk assessment to estimate future risks related to the IP to be transacted.*

Wen Xu:	In recent years, with the improvement of IP skills in Chinese enterprises, do you think professionals have more channels to obtain IP information?

Li: *More information channel, I think. I visit the websites of USPTO, UKIPO periodically. Besides, I also have visited certain websites the average Chinese IP lawyers would neglect, for example, I have visited Turkey Patent Office website. I have researched different countries' Trademark Law like Indian and Australian. Some famous companies in Shenzhen like ZTE or Huawei, have their own legal risk database, or would send their employees to Europe to observe on-site. Their experience has more or less been shared among Shenzhen IP circle because they have more in depth study on the issue.*

| **Wen Xu:** | Compared with several years ago, say in 2005, is there any difference that you deal with a warning letter or technical license agreement sent by a foreign company? |

Li: *Basically the same. Usually, Chinese company will not respond to such a warning letter to avoid confronting the opposite party directly. But that does not mean Chinese company will do nothing. Relevant analysis such as legal analysis, technical analysis, patent analysis and product relation analysis will be done simultaneously. We will study the attached technical license agreement carefully. Sometimes, we would accept and sign the license agreement. In addition, I will consider certain business factors. For example, if we have not started to sell the product or only sold very little, we will not care whether the other party brings a suit or not. If they want to sue, let them sue.*

| **Wen Xu:** | How do Chinese companies handle disputes related to trademarks and brands? |

Li: *I have engaged in trademark business for a long time, about 7-8 years, including international trademark registration, and trademark disputes involving foreign parties. When there is a trademark dispute, there are, usually, two solutions: one is through normal legal channel; the other is through negotiation, that is, we will send a settlement letter to the other party. We want to know each other first and seek an understanding to avoid litigation. Government shall support the brand development of Chinese companies. Brand can be long-lasting assets. Nowadays, the well known brands in China market are mostly western brands which has brought the western brand owners a lot money from China market. When developing our own brand, Chinese companies have encountered a series of issues both financial or non-financial which requires government support. . On one hand, the government shall establish a differentiating brand development policy; on the other hand, it needs to resolve excessive local protectionism in certain localities.*

Wen Xu:	What's the overseas IP strategy in next 5 years for COSHIP?

Li: *We hope that we can obtain positive cash return from company's overseas IP strategy in the next 5 years. We mainly take the COSHIP's overseas market development into consideration when we develop overseas IPR strategy. If our overseas market(s) do focus on Africa, instead of US, European, we will develop our trademark and copyright rather than patent because patent is useless in Africa. On the other hand, branding can establish recognition from local customers while copyright can reduce direct competition in the future. COSHIP's overseas IP strategy depends on our overseas business strategy. Currently, the main overseas IP issue of COSHIP is technology license from US and European parties, which needs to be resolved at present. We have not set forth specific limit for investment increase on overseas IP, as the most important factor is whether our investment will bring positive cash return.*

PART TWO

THE APPENDICES

HOT INTELLECTUAL PROPERTY CASES 2009-2010

CASE NO 1

Chint vs. Schneider, parties finally settled for the largest amount in China's patent litigation history.

April 15th, 2009 marks a historical day in China's patent litigation history. The French company Schneider settled its patent lawsuit with a Zhejiang company Chint at the beginning of the oral hearing conducted at the Zhejiang High People's Court. According to the settlement, Schneider ought to pay Chint monetary compensation in the amount of RMB157.5 million Yuan (approximately US$23 million) within fifteen days, otherwise Chint would have the right to apply for enforcement of the first instance judgment rendered by the Wenzhou Intermediate People's Court against Schneider in the amount of RMB334 million Yuan (approximately US$50 million).

On August 1, 2006, Chint filed a lawsuit in Wenzhou Intermediate People's Court against Schneider and its related parties for patent infringement asking for RMB500,000 Yuan (approximately US$80,000) in damages, a much lower demand in order for the case to be accepted by Wenzhou Court. Then in February 2007, six months later, Chint increased the damages demand to RMB334 million Yuan (approximately US$50 million), without transferring the case to the Zhejiang High People's Court.

The patent at issue, Chinese Patent No. ZL97248479.5 ('479 Patent), was a utility model patent, so called "petite patent" which was filed on November 11, 1997 and granted on June 2, 1999. The '479 Patent covered a high cutting off small circuit breaker with a ten-year validity expiring on November 10, 2007.

The case went through the Chinese Patent Re-examination Board (the "Patent Board") and the trial, almost in parallel with the trial court decision handed down first on September 29, 2007, ordered injunction and compensation in favour of Chint. Before the Zhejiang High People's Court's hearing, the Patent Board handed down a decision upholding the validity of the '479 Patent which did not go through substantive examination upon issuance. The case then settled, hoping to end the ten-year patent battle between the two companies worldwide.

CASE NO 2

Pfizer vs. Wellman, foreign plaintiff lost an extremely popular Chinese translation mark under the first to file regime.

On June 24, 2009, China's Supreme People's Court finally adjudicated that Pfizer lost a Chinese translation mark " 伟哥 "to Plaintiff Guangzhou Wellman Corp., ending an eleven-year legal battle.

In March 1998, Pfizer's Viagra blue pill came out, which was immediately covered by the Chinese media. Viagra was translated by the Chinese media as Weige "伟哥"meaning "great brother". But Pfizer did not choose "伟哥" as the trademark for the Chinese market, instead translating Viagra as Wanaike "万艾可"meaning "could have ten thousand lovers". With the increasing popularity of "伟哥", more than forty Chinese companies rushed to the Chinese Trademark Office ("CTMO") the same year to apply for "伟哥" trademark registration. One local company called Guangzhou Wellman Corp. won the lottery. When Pfizer realised the value of "伟哥", Wellman's "伟哥"trademark application was already accepted by the CTMO.

On June 22, 2002, "伟哥"mark was published and gazetted for public opposition. On day 89, just one day before the closure of the opposition period, Pfizer filed an opposition. On October 11, 2005, Pfizer filed a lawsuit against Wellman and other pharmaceutical companies claiming for well-known trademark infringement. The case went through Beijing No. 1 Intermediate People's Court, and Beijing High People's Court, finally the Supreme People's Court granted the certiorari to hear the case. The Court basically held that Pfizer has never used or promoted the Chinese mark "伟哥", and only Wellman had. Because China is a first to file regime, without establishing well known status by an unregistered mark before other's trademark filing date, whoever files first has the right to use the trademark. Pfizer could not establish "伟哥" was well known due to its use and promotion in China before 1998, thus, Wellman does not infringe Pfizer's right.

Interestingly, on April 8, 2009, the Chinese Trademark Review and Adjudication Board upheld Pfizer's trademark opposition which seems to be conflicting with the Court decision. It is yet to be seen whether Wellman will ultimately obtain the ownership of the mark.

CASE NO 3

Strix vs. Zhejiang JiaTai and Leqing FaDa, a British kettle company was awarded an "unprecedented" RMB 9.1 million Yuan (approximately US$1.3 million) compensation for patent infringement against Chinese small appliances manufacturers.

The case was filed in Beijing in December 2008 by Strix Ltd. - the world's leading manufacturer of electric kettle controls, against two electrical device makers - Zhejiang JiaTai Electrical Appliance Manufacture Co., Ltd. (JiaTai) and Leqing FaDa Electrical Appliance Co., Ltd. (FaDa), and two kettle manufacturers - Zhongshan WeiLing Electrical Appliance Co., Ltd. (WeiLing) and Zhongshan ShunLong Century Electrical Appliance Co., Ltd. (ShunLong), after Strix found that the companies were producing and selling electric control devices containing Strix's patented technology.

The patent in suit entitled "Liquid Heating Vessels" (ZL95194418.5) was filed by Strix through PCT on June 9, 1995 and covers a technology which automatically switches off electric kettles after the water has reached boiling point.

Although the defendant's manufacturing operations are in Guangzhou and Zhejiang, Strix chose to sue in Beijing for a better forum. To bring the lawsuit in Beijing, Strix has demonstrated that the infringing kettles, which were being sold across the country, were also available in Beijing.

In January 2010, the Beijing No. 1 Intermediate People's Court ruled that JiaTai and FaDa should stop producing and selling the two models of electric kettles containing such control devices, and pay damages of RMB 7.1 million Yuan (approximately US$1.04 million) and RMB 2 million Yuan (approximately US$ 294,000) respectively. While the majority of the damages were imposed on the control manufacturers, the court also ordered two kettle manufacturers- WeiLing and ShunLong, who were also involved in the case, to pay substantial damages and to stop the production and sale of two models of electric kettles containing those controls.

In this case, the compensation amount was calculated by the "infringer's illegal income", which is much higher than the maximum statutory damages awarded to the patent right holders.

CASE NO 4

Tomato Garden criminal case, copyright infringement of Microsoft Windows XP, where criminal liability was imposed.

The Tomato Garden version of Microsoft Windows XP program (Tomato Garden) was developed by Mr. Hong Lei who deciphered the program's authentication and certification barriers, enhanced the appearance of Windows XP desktop, buttons and certain program interface, and allowed users unrestricted access to certain Microsoft software. The use of Tomato Garden has been widespread in China and the program itself was ranked the second most popular operating system right after the original Windows XP.

Between December 2006 and August 2008, with the assistance of Mr. Hong Lei and other individual defendants, Chengdu Gongruan Network Technology Co., Ltd made various versions of Tomato Garden software, and provided access through public download at tomatolei.com and edudown.cn. While download was free of charge, the company made profit out of advertising. According to the judgment, Gongruan has an illegal income of RMB 2.92 million Yuan (approximately US$ 430,000).

Some defendants were arrested in 2008. On August 20, 2009, the Hu Qiu District People's Court in Su Zhou, Jiangsu Province, adjudicated that the defendants infringed the copyright of Microsoft, so the illegal income of Chengdu Gongruan should be seized and the company should be fined three times of its illegal income, that is, RMB 8.77 million Yuan (approximately US$1.23 million). Two principal individual defendants (including Mr. Hong Lei) were sentenced to jail for three and a half years and fined RMB 1 million Yuan (approximately US$ 147,000). Two subordinate criminal suspects were sentenced to jail for two years and fined RMB 100,000 Yuan (approximately US$ 14,700).

CASE NO 5

People vs. Tantian, the first trademark criminal case relating to 2010 Shanghai World Expo.

On October 16, 2009, Shanghai Pudong New District People's Court handed down a judgment of the first trademark criminal case relating to 2010 Shanghai World Expo.

Tantian was one of the defendants. In 2006, Tantian's mother paid for RMB 500,000 Yuan (approximately US$ 73,530) to establish

Changzheng Company (the other defendant in the present case; hereafter "Changzheng") pursuing metals and steel business. Tantian was the general manager of Changzheng and in charge daily work. In 2007, Chengzheng became a materials supplier to Shanghai Installation Engineering Co., Ltd. (hereafter "Installation Engineering. In July 2008, Installation Engineering was granted contracts of electrical installation work of certain Expo venues and Changzheng was responsible for supplying steel materials to Installation Engineering.

In December 2008, a man, named Mr. Chen, promoted to sell "Jinzhou" brand galvanized steel pipes to Changzheng. Tantian made a decision to buy ninety tons of these steel pipes with the price of RMB 456,000 Yuan (approximately US $ 67,059) which was obviously lower than the normal market price of "Jinzhou" brand steel pipes. Tantian sold these steel pipes to Installation Engineering for Expo venues buildings. In April 2009, Installation Engineering found that the steel pipes had breaking welding line when conducting random inspection to these steel pipes. Installation Engineering terminated Changzheng's supplier's qualification immediately and sent staff to carry out investigation. In order to verify the authenticity of steel pipes, Installation Engineering invited "Jinzhou" brand steel pipes manufacturer to conduct field verification. After verification by the manufacturer, these steel pipes were identified as counterfeit products. On May 6, 2009, Tantian turned himself into the public security department. On September 9, 2009, a public prosecution was instituted at the Pudong New District People's Court.

The court held that "Jinzhou and its logo" was a registered trademark in China. Jinzhou company was the owner of the registered trademark "Jinzhou and its logo" and their legitimate rights should be protected by law. Defendants, Changzheng and Tantian knowingly sold the products bearing fake trademark with a relatively large sales volume, which had not only infringed trademark right owned by Jinzhou Company, but also destroyed state trademark management system and disturbed the socialist market economic order. Their action had committed crime for selling goods bearing counterfeit registered trademark. Changzheng was a limited liability company which was established legally. Tantian was the general manager of Changzheng and in charge of company's business activities. Tantian signed steel pipe sale contract with Installation Engineering in the name of Changzheng and the earned profit belonging to Changzheng, which constituted enterprise crime under the Chinese Criminal Law . Tantian had repeatedly distributed genuine "Jinzhou" branded steel pipes and knew it well, but he purchased the steel pipes bearing counterfeit "Jinzhou" trademark with obvious low price and further forged certificate of product quality. The above facts specifically showed that Tantian wilfully sold the steel pipes bearing counterfeit "Jinzhou" trademark. Tantian, as the general manager of Changzheng, should bear the criminal liability according to the law.

The court decided that Changzheng committed crime for selling goods bearing counterfeit registered trademark and was punished with a fine of RMB 180,000 Yuan (approximately US $ 26,471); Tantian committed the same crime and was punished with imprisonment of two years and a fine of RMB 180,000 Yuan (approximately US $ 26,471); the seized steel pipes bearing counterfeit "Jinzhou" trademark were confiscated.

CASE NO 6

Wuhan Jingyuan vs. Japanese Fujikashui and Huayang, injunctive relief was not granted due to public interest consideration in an environmental sector IP infringement case.

On December 21, 2009, the Supreme People's Court adjudicated that Wuhan Jingyuan Environmental Project Tech Co., Ltd. (hereinafter Wuhan Jingyuan) won the patent infringement case against Japanese Fujikashui Engineering Co., Ltd. (hereinafter Japan FKK) and Huayang Electricity Co., Ltd. (hereinafter Huayang Company), ending an eight-year legal battle. Japan FKK and Huayang Company should jointly pay Wuhan Jingyuan RMB 50.6 million Yuan (approximately US$ 7.4 million), the largest patent compensation involving environmental products in China.

The patent in suit (ZL95119389.9) entitled Aeration Sea Water Type Technology for Removing Sulfur from Smoke and Aeration Device was filed by Wuhan Jingyuan in December 1995, and granted on September 25, 1999. The patent provides core technology to remove sulfur by using sea water, which is a substantial improvement and could reduce the cost by two thirds, compared with the traditional limestone sulfur removal process which consumes lots of more freshwater and energy.

The sulfur removal technology and equipment used by Huayang Company was provided by Japan FKK. According to the agreement between Huayang Company and Japan FKK, there is an indemnification clause stipulating that the Japan FKK should indemnify the Huayang Company for any losses, damages and fines relating to the patent rights of the equipment provided by Japan FKK.

On September 16, 2001, Wuhan Jingyuan initiated the patent infringement lawsuit before Fujian High People's Court. Subsequently, Japan FKK filed an invalidation request against the patent in suit before the Patent Board. During approximately six years of legal proceedings, Wuhan Jingyuan successfully defended the validity of the patent in suit before the Patent Board, Beijing Intermediate People's Court and Beijing High People's Court. On May 12, 2008, the Fujian High People's Court made its first instance judgment, ruling that: Japan FKK should cease the infringement and pay RMB 50.6 million Yuan (approximately US$ 7.4 million) to Wuhan Jingyuan for compensation and Huayang Company should pay certain royalty fees to Wuhan Jingyuan instead of injunction due to the public interest. The judgment was appealed to the Supreme People's Court. Then, Supreme People's Court made its final decision ruling that the defendants should jointly pay RMB50.6 million Yuan (approximately US$7.4 million) for the patent infringement.

CASE NO 7

Michelin Group vs. Tan Guoqiang and Ou Can, parallel import of goods without 3C approval was held to constitute an infringement of the trademark owner's right in China

On April 24, 2009, the Changsha Intermediate People's Court ruled that two individual tire dealers infringed the tire giant Michelin's trademark rights for selling Japanese-made Michelin tires in China without consent from the trademark owner and mandatory China Compulsory Product Certification (3C) approval. This case was regarded as the first trademark parallel import case in China by Chinese media.

The plaintiff, Michelin Group, is the trademark owner of Michelin series trademarks in China. In April 2008, Michelin engaged an agent to have bought Michelin brand tires with notary from the two tire dealers and then initiated the lawsuit seeking injunctive and monetary relief on February 22, 2009. It is notable that the tires in suit bear authentic Japanese-manufacturer Michelin's brand, but without the authorization for sale in China from Michelin. Moreover, the tire has not obtained 3C certification, which is mandatory before tires could be sold in China.

As the parallel imports of trademarked products is not specifically addressed in Chinese law and regulations, the Court focused on whether the sale of parallel imported products will constitute a trademark infringement if the sale in China is not authorized by the trademark right holder and the products do not comply with the 3C requirement. The Court found that the products in question should be inspected and certified in accordance with the 3C system before any import or sales in China market. Thus, the defendant's sales of such tires are illegal and should be forbidden. Further, the Court stated that if any quality or safety issue of the Japanese-made tires arises, the consumers will automatically relate this to Michelin. It is obvious that the defendant's unauthorized sales will damage Michelin's reputation, and then constitute an infringement of its trademark rights. The Court awarded an injunction against the sale of such products and a small amount of compensation to Michelin. The defendants did not appeal.

CASE NO 8

Siemens vs. Co-trust, seven patent infringement actions between the parties based on two Siemens invention patents, invalidity petitions filed before answer but the Court did not stay; interestingly the Court found infringement in two actions based on one patent but that patent later was declared invalid by the Patent Board; all cases are pending for appeal.

In 2009, seven patent lawsuits based on two patents between Siemens and Shenzhen Co-trust technology Co., Ltd. went to appeal before the Guangdong High People's Court. In the first instance, Siemens won two cases and lost five cases before the Shenzhen Intermediate People's Court.

The two patents in suit are Chinese patent ZL95197172.7 ('172 Patent), entitled "User Defined Prot and Protocol Scheme for a Programmable Logic Controller" and Chinese Patent ZL01814807.7 ('807 Patent), entitled "Universal Controller Expansion Module System, Method and Apparatus". These two invention patents filed by Siemens through PCT were granted in China in 2004 and 2006 respectively.

Between December 2007 and January 2008, Siemens accompanied by notary purchased several CPU devices and expansion module devices manufactured by Co-trust from certain distributors, then filed 7 lawsuits against Co-trust seeking injunctive relief and a monetary compensation in the amount of over RMB 17 million Yuan (approximately US$2.5 million). In answering the Complaint, Co-trust filed invalidation petitions to the Patent Board challenging the validity of the patents, but the Court did not stay the trial. During the, an expert report was provided by Beijing Zi Tu Forensic Sciences Center according to both parties' request. The expert report concluded that the accused CPU devices have the same features as the claimed ones of the '172 Patent but are not equivalent to the prior art references provided by Co-trust; and the accused expansion module devices have different technical solutions as the ones covered by the '807 Patent.

In November 2008, Shenzhen Intermediate People's Court made its first instance decision based on the expert report, adjudicating that Siemens won two lawsuits relating to the '172 Patent with a compensation of RMB 500,000 Yuan (approximately US$ 74,000) for each case, but rejected other five lawsuits relating to the '807 Patent.

Right after the Court's decision, the Patent Board declared that all claims of the '172 Patent invalid and partial claims of the '807 Patent invalid. Siemens then filed an appeal (administrative lawsuit) challenging Patent Board's decision before the Beijing No.1 Intermediate Court. Based on the Patent Board decision, Co-trust appealed the two cases it was ordered to pay to the Guangdong High People's Court based on the invalidity of the '172 Patent. Meanwhile, Siemens dissatisfied with the rejection of other five cases, also appealed to the same court based on the erroneous claim construction of the '807 Patent.

It will be a lengthy battle between the parties.

CASE NO 9

People vs. Bohai, a trade secret case where an employee stole and disclosed employer's trade secret, causing significant economic losses to employer and committing IP crime.

In September 2006, Tianjin Bohai Iron and Steel Engineering Technology Development Co, Ltd (hereafter "Bohai") was incorporated in Tianjin. After incorporation, Bohai signed a program design contract "AnGang High-performance Cold-rolled Silicon Steel Test Line Project" with AnGang Steel Company. In order to complete the program, Bohai recruited several design experts including Chu Naibing, Chen chunyuan and others who originally worked at WISDRI Engineering & Research Incorporation Limited (hereafter "WISDRI").

In March 2007, Bohai convened a regular meeting. At the meeting, Chu Naibing, Chen chunyuan and others proposed and decided to entrust Liu Xiang who worked at WISDRI to conduct design on two product lines of certain equipment with RMB 100,000 Yuan each (approximately US $ 14,706). After the meeting, Chen chunyuan contacted Liu Xiang directly and Liu Xiang agreed to design accordingly. Afterwards, Liu Xiang changed the drawing names, "TaiGang Cold-rolled Silicon Steel normalization-based Pickling Equipment Design Drawings" and "WuGang Two Silicon-oriented Silicon Steel Hot-drawing Formation Unit Equipment Design Drawings" both of which owned by WISDRI, into "High-performance Cold-rolled Silicon Steel Test Line Project". In addition, Liu Xiang changed the logo on the design drawings to Bohai's logo. Then, Liu Xiang delivered the design drawing to Bohai by Chen chunyuan and received RMB 150,000 Yuan (approximately US $ 22,059) paid by Bohai as a reward.

On September 14, 2009, Wuhan Jianghan District People's court made the first instance judgment. The court held: Bohai used high rewards to induce Liu Xiang to steal and disclose WISDRT's trade secret and used WISDRT's trade secret into its AnGang program directly; Chen chuanyuan, Chu Naibing and others, as Bohai's management, directly involved in obtaining WISDRT's trade secret by unfair method such as inducement; Liu xiang violated confidentiality agreement signed between Liu xiang and WISDRI. The action of Bohai, Chen chunyuan, Chu Naibing, and Liu Xiang caused significant economic losses to the trade secret owner-WISDRI.

The first instance court held that Bohai committed trade secret crime and was sentenced to a fine of RMB 1.6 million Yuan (approximately US $ 235,294); Liu xiang and Chen chunyuan committed trade secret crime and were sentenced to imprisonment for two years and a fine of RMB 800,000 Yuan (approximately US $ 117,647)respectively. Chu Naibing committed trade secret crime and was sentenced to imprisonment for ten months and fourteen days and a fine of RMB 800,000 Yuan (approximately US $ 117,647). All the defendants were not satisfied with the judgment of the first instance court and appealed. On January 5, 2010, Wuhan Intermediate People's court rejected the defendants' appeal and affirmed the judgment of the first instance.

CASE NO 10

Exxon Mobil vs. American Mobil International Petroleum Group, registration of internet keyword and domain name may constitute trademark infringement. The infringing internet keyword and domain names were cancelled.

On July 24, 2009, Shanghai Intermediate People's Court made its first instance decision in a trademark infringement and unfair competition action brought by Exxon Mobil against American Mobil International

Petroleum Group, a Hong Kong registered company, Xi'an Yanqing Technology Development Co., and Shanghai Songjing Industrial Co. The Court held that the defendants infringed Exxon Mobil's trademark right and engaged in unfair competition due to their registration and misuse of certain internet keyword and domain names, thus awarded Exxon Mobil an injunction and a monetary compensation RMB 500,000 Yuan (approximate US$ 73,209).

Exxon Mobil is the owner of trademark "美孚", which is the Chinese translation for "Mobil" and widely known by relevant public in China. The defendants registered an internet keyword - "美国美孚石油" (American Mobil Petroleum) and two Chinese domain names - "美国美孚石油.中国" and "美国美孚石油.cn" in China. The internet keyword and domain names include Exxon Mobil's Chinese trademark. The Court held that due to the distinctiveness of the two Chinese characters "美孚" in the keyword and domain names, the Chinese characters used in the internet keyword and domain names are similar to Exxon Mobil's Chinese trademark. Because such similarity will confuse consumers to assume certain relationship between the defendants and Exxon Mobil, the defendant infringed Exxon Mobil's trademark right by registering and using similar internet keyword and domain names. The Court further ordered the defendants to cancel the registration of the internet keyword and domain names.

In addition, the Court held that the defendants' conduct constituted unfair competition because they have caused customer's confusion, utilized Exxon Mobil's reputation and breached the business ethics.

CASE EXTRA

Sohu ChangYou vs. Beijing Kylin, an online game copyright case where plaintiff increased damages amount from RMB 1 Yuan to RMB 19 millions Yuan (approximately US $ 2.8 millions) during the suit.

Sohu ChangYou, a NASDAQ listed company, filed a lawsuit against Beijing Kylin Network Information Technology Co.,Ltd. (hereafter "Kylin") for infringement on the copyright of Sohu ChangYou's online game "Dragon Oath " at Beijing Haidian District People's Court on July 7, 2009. Sohu ChangYou alleged that the online games "Genghis Khan" developed and operated by Kylin had copied certain programs of Dragon Oath.

The plaintiff alleged that the defendant's CEO and its main team were former employees of Sohu ChangYou who had involved in the development of Dragon Oath and had access to the codes of Dragon

Oath. Therefore, the defendant has infringed plaintiff's copyright. Sohu ChangYou requested the court to order the defendant to stop running online game "Genghis Khan" immediately, stop copying and transmitting "Genghis Khan" to online users, offer public apology, and pay RMB 1 Yuan as compensation.

On October 19, 2009, the judges in charge of the case went to Kylin to carry out evidence preservation. Based on the evidence disclosed by Sohu ChangYou, at least from the client server, Kylin's "Genghis Khan" was almost the same as Dragon Oath. Further, the client server of "Genghis Khan" even contained certain identical BUGs of the earlier version Dragon Oath. Kylin argued this was because both "Genghis Khan" and "Dragon Oath" used the US open-source engine Ogre. After the evidence preservation, Sohu ChangYou filed an application at the court to raise the compensation demand from RMB 1 Yuan to RMB 19 millions Yuan (approximately US $ 2.8 millions). The case is still pending.

HOT INTELLECTUAL PROPERTY ISSUES 2009-2010

CHINA'S HIGHEST COURT OPINES ON IMPLEMENTATION OF NATIONAL INTELLECTUAL PROPERTY STRATEGY: COURTS URGED TO PROTECT THE INTERESTS OF INTELLECTUAL PROPERTY RIGHTS HOLDERS

On March 30, 2009, the Supreme People's Court (SPC) of the People's Republic of China (PRC), China's highest court, issued its Opinions on the Implementation of the National Intellectual Property Strategy (Opinion). The Opinion provides the framework for effectively implementing within the court system the National Intellectual Property Strategy Outlines (Strategy) published by the State Counsel on June 5, 2008. The Opinion, which re-emphasizes the importance of intellectual property rights (IPR) and seeks to enhance the judicial protections of such rights, is therefore likely to affect the protection of IPR in China significantly.

Pursuant to the Opinion, China's judicial bodies shall take a leading role in intellectual property (IP) protection, thereby contributing to China's transformation into an "innovation-oriented nation," one of the central tenets of the PRC government's most recent five-year plan. Specifically, the SPC urges all courts to utilize actively comprehensive remedies to protect the interests of IPR holders, including both monetary and non-monetary remedies. In addition, the SPC particularly encourages all courts to enhance damages awards in IP-infringement cases, especially for those with serious circumstances (i.e., willful infringement) so as to effectively prevent repeated infringement by the same infringer(s) and more widespread infringement. Finally, the Opinion also states that it will (1) expedite the establishment of a quasi-precedential reporting system for IP-related cases in order to unify judgment standards; (2) intensify the judicial re-examination of the activities of granting and affirming IPR by administrative authorities in order to unify the examination standards for grant of IPR; and (3) promote the publication of all IP-related court decisions.

While general guidance on handling various IPR infringement cases has been provided, the Opinion also emphasizes the balance between

IP protection and public interest, and cautions against the abuse of IPR. For instance, the SPC's Opinion notes that (1) the scope of a patent claim should be interpreted accurately and the doctrine of equivalents should be applied more narrowly; (2) well-known trademarks shall be recognized passively and prudently by the courts on both a case-by-case and a need-to-have basis; (3) in trade secret cases, the courts also shall protect the alleged infringer's own trade secrets from being inappropriately acquired by the plaintiff; (4) the courts shall be very cautious when adopting pre-litigation interim measures for invention and utility model patent cases (i.e., injunctive remedies), though for trademark and copyright infringement cases, the interim measures shall be adopted more actively; and (5) acts constituting unfair competition shall be recognized based on the Anti-Unfair Competition Law's general principle that "market competitors shall not violate the principle in good faith and honesty" and shall not be made simply on the ground of utilizing or damaging competitive advantage.

The SPC notes its intention to study carefully the necessity and possibility of establishing a special unified IPR tribunal to address civil, administrative, and criminal IPR cases as well as an IP appeal court, although no further details have been provided in this Opinion.

With respect to legislation, the SPC states in the Opinion that it very soon will issue the Judicial Interpretations on Protections of Well-Known Trademarks and in the very near future will roll out the Judicial Interpretations on Patent Infringement Assessment Standard and the Judicial Interpretations on Civil Procedures for Anti-Monopoly Lawsuits. Considering the technical aspects of many IP cases, the SPC also will establish certain legal procedures concerning judicial appraisals, expert witnesses, and technical investigations, among other issues.

In summary, the Opinion provides general guidance to all PRC courts in terms of IPR protections and touches on several important issues relating to such protections in China. With the issuance of such an Opinion, enhanced IPR protections and more uniform and transparent court decisions can be expected.

CHINA'S HIGHEST COURT OPINION ADDRESSES IMPACT OF THE INTERNATIONAL FINANCIAL CRISIS ON INTELLECTUAL PROPERTY[2]

In the face of the international financial crisis, China continues to focus on the importance of intellectual property (IP). On April 21, 2009, China's highest court — the Supreme People's Court of the People's Republic of China (PRC) — issued its Opinion on Certain Issues With Respect to Intellectual Property Judicial Adjudication Under the Current Economic Situation (Opinion) within the court system in China.

The Opinion, among various other issues, provides explicit guidance as follows:

- That courts shall strictly apply the doctrine of equivalents to avoid inappropriate broadening of patent scope

- That prior use rights shall be reasonably recognized in patent lawsuits

- That the courts shall recognize defenses based on prior art (the doctrine of which has been codified into the Third Amendment to the PRC Patent Law; See

- http://www.foley.com/publications/pub_detail.aspx?pubid=5766)

- That courts shall recognize well-known trademarks under strict conditions based on necessity.

- That courts shall appropriately balance between trade secret protection (including non-compete issues) and employee career development.

- That courts shall improve the system for declaratory judgments of non-infringement in order to restrain abuse of IP rights

- That courts shall be cautious in issuing pre-suit preliminary injunctions.

- That courts shall explore the possibility of relying upon experts such as accountants, auditors, and professional evaluation agencies when deciding damages.

---

[2] A full Chinese version of the Opinion is available at:
http://news.xinhuanet.com/legal/2009-04/24/content_11247180.htm

Consistent with the National Intellectual Property Strategy Outlines published by the State Counsel on June 5, 2008, the Opinion emphasizes the balance between IP protection and public interests, and will certainly impact the protection of IP rights in China.

JUDICIAL RECOGNITION OF WELL-KNOWN TRADEMARKS IN CHINA MAY BE TIGHTENED UP

On April 23, 2009, the PRC Supreme People's Court (SPC) issued its Judicial Interpretation of Several Issues Regarding Application of Laws in Well-Known Trademark-Protection-Related Civil Disputes (Interpretation). The Interpretation addresses various issues relating to well-known trademark recognition that have surfaced since the Provisions for the Determination and Protection of Well-Known Trademarks were issued by the State Administration for Industry and Commerce on June 1, 2003 (2003 Provisions). The Interpretation became effective on May 1, 2009.

The Interpretation, when implemented, is likely to reshape the judicial scheme for recognition of well-known trademarks set forth by the 2003 Provisions. Proposed changes include the following: (1) causes of actions for recognition of well-known status will be limited to trademark infringement and unfair competition claims recognized under applicable law, excluding (a) trademark or unfair competition claims not explicitly recognized under applicable law or (b) cases where the well-known status of the mark has no material bearing on the outcome of the case; (2) the well-known status will not be confirmed by the principal text of a court judgment or in writing in a court-administered settlement adjudication, which will prevent the res judicata doctrine from applying for future cases; and (3) trademark holders and owners will bear the burden of proof of establishing well-known status, and courts should not make a well-known determination based solely on the alleged infringer's admission, to prevent, in part, potential conspired phony lawsuits designed to establish the well-known status of certain marks.

Notably, the issued Interpretation omitted at least one key provision from the draft circulated on November 11, 2008. Specifically, the Interpretation omitted the well-known status of the mark outside China as a factor in recognizing well-known status in China. Thus, the Interpretation confirms that the 2003 Provisions will continue to define Chinese and China, respectively, to be the relevant public and relevant geography in determining well-known status. Another key change is that the domain name will be difficult to use as the basis for a cause of action for well-known trademark recognition. The Interpretation defines only (1) the domain name contains the well-known trademark or its similarity; (2) the relevant products are traded under the domain name through e-commerce; and (3) it will mislead the relevant general public, then one can raise the infringement case with recognition of well-known trademark.

Furthermore, under the SPC's January 9, 2009 Notification on Jurisdiction Issues Regarding Well-Known Trademark Recognition Related Civil Disputes, only certain courts at the intermediate level or above located in provincial capitals or other designated cities have the jurisdiction over cases for determining well-known trademark status.

In view of these changes, it appears that the PRC courts are likely to limit judicial recognition of well-known trademark in the future.

▪ CHINA MARCHES TOWARD THIRD REVISION OF TRADEMARK LAW: NEW DRAFT AMENDMENTS SIGNAL POTENTIAL EASE OF SURVEILLANCE BURDEN ON OWNERS

The current era of intellectual property reform in China is impacting both patent and trademark law alike. China is in the process of revising — for the third time — its Trademark Law, which was first promulgated on August 23, 1982. Unlike the second amendment to the PRC Trademark Law, adopted in preparation of China's accession to the World Trade Organization in 2001, the current third revision was initiated by the China Trademark Office (CTMO) to streamline the trademark prosecution and enforcement process to meet the demand of rapid domestic economic growth. On June 20, 2009, the State Administration for Industry and Commerce (SAIC) issued a revised draft of the proposed amendments to the PRC Trademark Law (2009 Draft Amendments). The 2009 Draft Amendments are significant, as they represent changes currently contemplated in an ongoing process to reshape the law governing brand procurement and protection in China. It is anticipated that the third amendment will be finalized and implemented within the next two years.

Chinese trademark policy is presently a dynamic area of change. The 2009 Draft Amendments come on the heels of the May 1, 2009 implementation of the Judicial Interpretation of Several Issues

Regarding Application of Laws in Well-Known Trademark-Protection-Related Civil Disputes (Interpretation) issued by the PRC Supreme People's Court. [See Foley's June 11, 2009 Legal News Alert: China, "Judicial Recognition of Well-Known Trademarks in China May Be Tightened Up," at http://www.foley.com/publications/pub_detail.aspx?pubid=6100.] The Interpretation addresses various issues related to well-known trademark recognition that have surfaced since the Provisions for the Determination and Protection of Well-Known Trademarks were issued by the SAIC on June 1, 2003.

The 2009 Draft Amendments retain features similar to those previously presented in a draft last circulated for comment in August 2007 (2007 Draft). [See Foley's June 11, 2009 article, "China Trademark Law Is Being Revised: Is the Third Time Really a Charm?" at http://www.foley.com/publications/pub_detail.aspx?pubid=6096#5.] Specifically, the 2009 Draft Amendments provide for a scope of registrable trademarks to include color marks and non-visual marks such as sounds, smells, and motion marks. Notably, the examination and registration procedures for marks will be addressed in regulations to be separately promulgated by the SAIC. The 2009 Draft Amendments allow for multi-class applications and propose to double the present limit for maximum statutory damages to RMB 1 million (currently about U.S. $147,000). In addition, the 2009 Draft Amendments provide for increased administrative fines of up to five times the amount of the illegal gain and, where the illegal gain cannot be quantified, the maximum statutory fine may reach RMB 1 million (about U.S. $147,000). Also, standing to file trademark oppositions and invalidation actions would be restricted to parties holding prior rights and interested parties. Notably, the 2009 Draft Amendments do not define "interested parties."

The 2009 Draft Amendments retain features of the 2007 Draft that serve to enhance enforcement of owners' rights in either registered or unregistered marks. For example, the 2009 Draft Amendments provide for enforcement rights where "the principle of honesty and credibility" has been violated. As such, separate from the Anti-Unfair Competition Law, the PRC Trademark Law would provide a potential protection for owners of unregistered trademarks against the knowing pre-emptive registrations of other parties. The 2009 Draft Amendments also provide a remedy in favor of select marks that are not recognized as "well-known" trademarks. In present practice, only well-known trademarks can have the cross-class protection, but the well-known trademark status is difficult to obtain. It is nearly impossible for most foreign brand owners to protect their trademarks from "bad-will" copy registrations in other classes. Significantly, the 2009 Draft Amendments provide cross-class protection for trademarks having certain significance in China but that are not yet well known. As a result, many foreign brand owners would likely benefit from this expansion of cross-class protection.

The 2009 Draft Amendments have been revised in several important areas in relation to the 2007 Draft. First, the 2009 Draft Amendments no longer require the CTMO to complete the examination of trademarks within 12 months of the date of application filing. The 2007 Draft proposed to set a statutory one-year examination term for trademark applications. This was a very ambitious proposal in view of the increased volume of applications and significant backlog for pending cases. Second, the 2007 Draft proposal shifted the burden of "gate keeping" before and after the applications to applicants and registrants. In the 2009 Draft Amendments, substantive examination of a candidate mark by the CTMO for refusal based on relative grounds has been maintained. Retention of this requirement may serve to ease significantly the burden on trademark owners to monitor the marketplace for and file oppositions against confusingly similar marks.

The ascendance of the Chinese marketplace as a global powerhouse serves to heighten international interest in changes implemented during this period of intellectual property reform in China. The 2009 Draft Amendments provide insight into the potential changes to Chinese trademark law that will set the tone for future brand creation, management, and protection in this important market.

KEY PROVISIONS OF PRC JUDICIAL INTERPRETATION ON PATENT INFRINGEMENT TO TAKE EFFECT ON JANUARY 1, 2010

On December 21, 2009, the PRC Supreme People's Court adopted several provisions of the Supreme People's Court on Issues Concerning Applicable Laws to the Trial of Patent Infringement Controversies (Judicial Interpretation). The Judicial Interpretation draws from and parallels the implementation of last year's Third Amendment to the Patent Law, and will become effective as of January 1, 2010. A Chinese version is available at

http://www.chinacourt.org/flwk/show.php?file_id=140350.

In July 2009, Foley reported the circulation of a draft Judicial Interpretation (Draft) for public comments. (See http://www.foley.com/publications/pub_detail.aspx?pubid=6159.) As compared to the Draft, the final Judicial Interpretation is a simplified version and provides a more general guideline that gives PRC courts more discretion on a variety of complex issues. A summary of the final Judicial Interpretation follows.

Scope of Protection

A significant portion of the Judicial Interpretation concerns the determination of the scope of patent protection.

Claim Construction

Specifically, the Judicial Interpretation sets forth that the court will/should determine the scope of patent protection based on recitation of the claims, in combination with an understanding of the claims by an ordinarily skilled person in the art upon his/her reading of the specification and drawings (Section 2).

Narrow Interpretation for "Means" Claims

The Judicial Interpretation also provides for narrow interpretation of means-plus-function claims, similar to the United States (35 USC §112, ¶ 6).

However, during prosecution, most patent examiners currently read the means-plus-function claims broadly to cover all possible mechanisms that perform the same function. Such examination practice is likely to change in light of the Judicial Interpretation.

All Elements Rule

The Judicial Interpretation also explicitly requires that all technical features or their equivalents shall be present in the accused infringing product for a finding of patent infringement (Section 7). This essentially abandons the widely criticized "superfluity establishing principle," which was adopted by the Beijing High People's Court in an earlier decision. There, the court considered a feature of an independent claim apparently "non-essential" and removed it from consideration when determining infringement.

Prosecution History Estoppel

The Judicial Interpretation indicates that, if during prosecution or invalidity proceedings, a patent applicant or patent holder abandoned certain technical solutions through amendments or response(s), the scope of protection shall exclude such abandoned subject matter(s) (Section 6). Noticeably, unlike the Draft, the Judicial Interpretation does not require the amendments or responses to be "restrictive," which appears to suggest that such estoppel theory may have a broader application.

Design Patent Infringement

For design patents, the Judicial Interpretation abandoned the "relevant public" concept introduced in the Draft. Instead, the Judicial Interpretation reiterates that identicalness or similarity of designs shall be determined in accordance with the knowledge and recognition of a general consumer (Section 10).

Prior Art Defense

The Third Amendment to the Patent Law codifies the doctrine of prior art defense, under which the PRC courts may find no infringement if the defendant has evidence to prove that his/her technology or design is covered by or performed in accordance with prior art or prior art design. The Judicial Interpretation requires the reliance upon one piece of prior art (or design) in such a defense, but also allows certain changes from the cited prior art. For example, with respect to utility patents, the features of the accused infringing product can be "not substantially different from" those of the prior art; with respect to design patents, the design of the accused infringing product can be "not substantially different from" that of the prior art.

Cease and Desist Letters

The Judicial Interpretation sets forth that the accused infringer is entitled to file a declaratory judgment if the patentee — within one month after receipt of, or within two months after dispatch of, written notice from the accused infringer who has received a cease and desist letter therefrom, urging the patentee to take legal actions — fails to withdraw this letter or to bring a lawsuit. Such an additional procedural requirement may give the patentee significant advantages over the accused infringer in terms of forum shopping.

Noticeable Removals From the Draft

Various sections have been removed from the Draft. For example, the assembling and recycle and contributory infringement sections have been removed, probably due to controversies that became apparent during the comment period. Sections regarding doctrine of equivalents and patents adopted in industrial standards also have been deleted, probably for the reason that such issues have been addressed in previous judicial interpretations (which remain effective) or will be further addressed in pending legislation activities.

Conclusion

The Judicial Interpretation is particularly important, as it represents a powerful interpretative tool for Chinese patent law and practice. Nevertheless, the Judicial Interpretation remains silent on a number of complex and controversial issues. It is possible that the PRC Supreme People's Court may seek to provide further guidance on such issues by agreeing to hear certain cases in the future, which we will certainly monitor closely.

PRC'S SIPO ISSUES NEW IMPLEMENTATION REGULATION IN ASSOCIATION WITH ITS THIRD AMENDMENT TO PATENT LAW

On January 9, 2010, the State Council of the People's Republic of China (PRC) finally approved the long-awaited new Implementation Regulation of the Patent Law (Implementation Regulation), which primarily addresses procedural issues in connection with the recent changes to PRC Patent Law. The Implementation Regulation will become effective on February 1, 2010, and a Chinese version is available at

http://www.gov.cn/zwgk/2010-01/18/content_1513398.htm.

Certain important amendments are discussed in this alert.

National Security Review Procedure

In connection with the newly introduced national security review, applicants seeking to file either in a foreign country or a Patent Cooperation Treaty (PCT) application with a foreign receiving office must provide a detailed description of the invention together with the filing of a request for national security review, regardless of whether or not a Chinese application has been filed. The SIPO is required (1) to inform the applicant within four months of the filing of the request if it believes that a national security review is necessary, and (2) to decide within six months whether or not the invention relates to national security such that it shall be kept confidential. If within the four- or six-month statutory period the SIPO has not responded, favorable decisions are assumed, and the applicant is free to file the foreign or PCT patent application.

Furthermore, the filing of a PCT application with SIPO is tantamount to filing a request for a national security review. The Implementation Regulation fails to provide any further details about how the review will be conducted in such a scenario. More guidance is expected from the Guidelines for Examination, which are still being reviewed by SIPO, the current draft of which appears to suggest a shorter confidentiality review period, as we reported in our previous legal alert:

http://www.foley.com/publications/pub_detail.aspx?pubid=6421.

The new Implementation Regulation merely provides a vague definition of "invention or utility model made in China"; that is, inventions where substantive contents of the technical solution are accomplished in China. As such, uncertainties exist with respect to inventions made through international cooperation.

Invalidation Grounds Expanded

The new Implementation Regulation has expanded the grounds for invalidating an issued patent in accordance with the new PRC Patent Law. Two major new invalidation grounds include (1) the violation of the national security review requirement by the applicant, and (2) the illegal obtaining or use of genetic resources to complete the invention-creation.

In addition, applicants have a duty to disclose the use of genetic resources during prosecution of an application, and no patent will be granted if an applicant does not comply with this duty. However, failure to disclose is not a ground to invalidate an issued patent.

Inventor Reward and Remuneration

Most significantly, the PRC Patent Law entitles the inventor to receive monetary rewards and remuneration, which remuneration can be represented by a certain percentage of the license fees or the patentee's profits that result from exploitation of the patented technology.

Standards of such rewards and remuneration set forth in the current implementation regulation are applicable only to PRC state-owned entities. However, under the new Implementation Regulation, such standards also would be applicable to private entities, unless it is otherwise decided in the company policy or individual contract. Companies with operations in China, especially R&D activities, should strongly consider taking appropriate steps in advance of the effective date to prepare for this change.

Significant Changes Relating to Multiple-Design Patents

Under the new PRC Patent Law, applicants may file a multiple-design application for more than one similar design of the same product. Accordingly, the new Implementation Regulation provides that (1) the applicant shall identify one primary design in the brief description, and (2) not more 10 similar designs can be included in one multiple-design application.

The new Implementation Regulation clarifies a number of issues raised by the Third Amendment to the PRC Patent Law and provides those in the intellectual property field with more guidance on various procedures, though some uncertainties remain.

INDEX